The Winter Garden Photograph   Reina

The Winter Garden Photograph

Reina María Rodríguez

Translated from the Spanish
by Kristin Dykstra
with Nancy Gates Madsen

Ugly Duckling Presse, 2019

The Winter Garden Photograph
© Reina María Rodríguez, 2019
Translation © Kristin Dykstra, 2019
Introduction © Kristin Dykstra, 2019
Interview © Rosa Alcalá, 2019

Originally published as *La foto del invernadero*
(Havana: Fondo Editorial Casa de las Américas, 1998)

ISBN 978-1-946433-22-0

First Edition, First Printing, 2019
Edition of 800

Ugly Duckling Presse
The Old American Can Factory
232 Third Street #E-303
Brooklyn, NY 11215
www.uglyducklingpresse.org

Distributed by SPD/Small Press Distribution, Inpress Books (UK),
and Raincoast Books (Canada) via Coach House Books

Images from the author's archives.
Design and typesetting by Silvina López Medin, Jamie Chiang, and Don't Look Now!
The type is Bell MT and Bell Centennial Std

Books printed offset and bound at McNaughton & Gunn
Cover printed offset by Prestige Printing

This book was published with the support of the New York State Council on the Arts.

table of contents

Prologue: Frozen Frames

This book opens with a command: "See."

The poems following it assemble acts of observation. To compose her title poem, Reina María Rodríguez considered a phrase from an essay by Roland Barthes.[1] Barthes tries to understand his late mother's life and identity by examining family photographs. In the process he expresses frustration and a lack of faith in photography's ability to capture reality. Yet when he arrives at one image, the winter garden photograph—a picture of his mother as a child, standing by a conservatory—it brings him a special sense of intimacy with his mother, in spite of all his doubts.

Rodríguez's own fascination with images led her to extended reflections on sight, desire, and loss. She followed Barthes's lead in contemplating photography through the lens of language. Flipping through the pages of UNESCO's magazine *Courier* at her rooftop home in Havana, she juxtaposed its international scenes with images of her home and the objects to be found there.

It took me many years to find the forgotten source of the epigraph Rodríguez placed before her poems, summoning readers to see.[2] She took it from a 1988 essay in *Courier* by French poet Yves Bonnefoy, whose search for compassion in the processes and products of photography leads him to admit that photography all too often pairs its care with cruelty. But like Barthes, he finds reason for hope.

---

1   *Camera Lucida: Reflections on Photography.* Tr. Richard Howard. NY: Hill and Wang, 1981. 71.

2   A Colombian magazine eventually republished the Spanish-language version of the essay online. I found it in *Rinoceronte 14: Revista Digital de Arte y Literatura* (www.rinoceronte14.org, n.d.).

Martine Franck becomes his example of the rare artist who succeeds in creating a compassionate enlightenment. Silent, intuitive, Franck is an "alchemist," the magician who transforms all evidence of relative realities into the impossible gold of a shared meaning: a glimpse of absolute truth, one surpassing human contestations. Franck becomes the antidote to the "kind of cruelty that is sometimes passed off as a desire to seek truth" with the camera lens—cruelty, Bonnefoy insists, because photographers too often undercut their penetrating vision with emotional blindness.[3]

Rodríguez takes her poems into these contradictions involved in bearing witness through the creation of imagery. Love, sensuality, and friendship give warmth to many scenes. Yet when she looks at the book in retrospect, Rodríguez emphasizes that she sees detachment rather than synthesis at the emotional center of these poems. She says, "Landscapes get erased; they deteriorate; they're purely 'intellectualized,' so to speak. They're cold."[4] For Rodríguez this detachment represents a fundamental flaw in her polished book.

Yet the imagery of cracks is relevant, humane in its very failure. It conjures many kinds of emotional and social breakage. Two examples: a fracture between social roles and the individuals who try but can't completely fit into them; or, the inconsistent meanings of objects we collect in order to symbolize what we want to be. There's something deceptive about the quiet atmosphere of *The Winter Garden Photograph*. It is not a complacent or quietist book, but a challenging one. The poetry presents us with a mind detaching itself from its surroundings, taking stock.

3   Bonnefoy, Yves. "The compassionate eye." UNESCO Courier (April 1988): 8.
    General Reference Center GOLD (accessed February 10, 2019). http://link.
    galegroup.com.library.smcvt.edu/apps/doc/A6354160/GRGM?u=vol_b92st-
    m&sid=GRGM&xid=d55717c7. 8.

4   "Desire for Something that Doesn't Exist: Interview Between Reina María
    Rodríguez and Kristin Dykstra." *How2* I.7 (Spring 2002). Archived online at
    Arizona State University / The Piper Center: < https://www.asu.edu/pipercw-
    center/how2journal/archive/online_archive/v1_7_200/current/translation/dyk-
    strainterview.htm >.

As Rodríguez wrote the collection, she was also reflecting in daily journal notes on the seismic shifts transforming many different levels of her life. Her archived notebooks, journals, and letters show how those meditations became poems. Physically, Rodríguez was suffering from a painful illness that made sexual activity difficult and probably dangerous. Her relationship with her long-term partner was in crisis, and their everyday life included tense negotiation. Also in crisis was her self-image as someone who had given birth to four children and was reimagining herself as a woman past childbearing age. She remained interested in sexuality and in sensuality but found herself forced to redefine what these experiences might be. For the purposes of writing, for example, exploring sensuality meant transforming writers of interest into imagery of painted and sculpted male beauty in her poems, marking these frozen men as inaccessible. Meanwhile her literary reputation continued to grow throughout the '90s, which aggravated dissonance with her partner. These personal concerns bleed through the fractured intimacies of her poems.[5]

A constant characteristic of Rodríguez's writing is her ability to connect apparently private reflections to the broader life of her community. Social pressures inform the tensions in *The Winter Garden Photograph* in muted yet significant ways. During the mid- to late 1990s, the city of Havana and the nation of Cuba had moved well into crisis. The ongoing economic embargo by the United States merged with ongoing fallout from global realignments around the former Soviet Union, which had long offered a variety of important partnerships and resources to Cuba. While the island's leadership sought to hold onto its identity, accomplishments, and forms of organization in post-1959 society, broader

---

5   The Princeton University Library holds the Reina María Rodríguez Papers, which
      include pieces of notebooks from the time of composition of *La foto del invernadero*.
      My remarks on the author's personal life and its flow into her writing refer to
      movements on the pages of those notebooks, as well as to our past conversations.
      This introduction incorporates selected segments from a longer article I pub-
      lished in a scholarly journal, regarding the contexts and composition of the book:
      "'A Just Image': Poetic Montage and Cuba's Special Period in *The Winter Garden
      Photograph*." *Mosaic: A Journal for the Interdisciplinary Study of Literature* 41.2 (2008):
      55–74.

global shifts re-contextualized the island's ability to operate in the world at large. Its internal economy declined precipitously. The island had entered its "Special Period" of crisis and forced transformation. Its changes permeated the fabric of everyday life, affecting Cubans' sense of place in world history.

The Winter Garden Photograph registers seismic movements through the expression of crisis in personal interfaces with the speakers' surroundings. "All human beings act within certain culturally shaped background expectations and understandings, often not conscious, about what 'reality' is," writes Katherine Verdery, showing that the late twentieth century is characterized in post-Soviet societies by a crisis in the "general understanding of their place in the universe."[6] Among elements of that general understanding fall broad concerns about community origins and identity, accompanied by questions of different scope: "What makes conduct moral or immoral; what are the essential attributes of a 'person'; what is time, and how does it flow (or not)".

Verdery's last example about the flow of time is particularly relevant to *The Winter Garden Photograph*. The same question animates these poems, with their speakers mulling over the construction of time. Some poems focus on gestures of the moment (an elderly woman bending over in a plaza), others on postures of frozen eternity (a speaker imagines herself embracing statues under the sea; a diver hangs suspended above the water). One poem explores one of the world's most famous photographs, an image of Ernesto "Che" Guevara shot in 1960, wondering about its legacy for the present. Meditations on the nature of time and reality act as triggers, opening out into profound disturbances and reconstructions of meaning in everyday life.

Rodríguez portrays human relationships with objects in these portraits of moments she extracts from life. Objects anchor daily human activities, giving form to domestic landscapes. They give concrete definition

---

6   *The Political Lives of Dead Bodies: Reburial and Postsocialist Change.* NY: Columbia University Press, 1999. 34.

to abstract aspects of place. Rodríguez read avidly while composing her book and drew on related ruminations by other writers—among them Virginia Woolf, to whom Rodríguez has often turned. Of objects and their alignments with one's consciousness Woolf writes, "Looked at again and again half consciously by a mind thinking of something else, any object mixes itself so profoundly with the stuff of thought that it loses its actual form and recomposes itself a little differently in an ideal shape which haunts the brain when we least expect it."[7] Rodríguez pursues this haunting of the mind by objects, one of her methods for making everyday life simultaneously recognizable yet oddly unfamiliar.

The Winter Garden Photograph was immediately recognized as a powerful book in Latin America. It won the prestigious Casa de las Américas international prize for poetry in 1998—the second time Rodríguez had taken that prize, cementing her reputation as a writer of the highest order.

While the book symbolizes a certain kind of closure to the twentieth century, it is far from marking the end of Rodríguez's own writing. She continues to be known for her stark dedication to artistic integrity. Her daily involvement in writing has translated into a stream of well-regarded works of poetry and prose in the twenty-first century. Among other awards, she received Cuba's National Prize for Literature in 2013, followed by the international acclaim of the 2014 Pablo Neruda Ibero-American Poetry Award, an extraordinary mark of respect in the Spanish-language literary world.

---

7   From "Solid Objects." *The Complete Shorter Fiction of Virginia Woolf.* NY: Harcourt & Brace, 1985. 104.

Regarding the Translation

The translation of this book began with a dozen co-translated poems. Most are now published in a bilingual anthology,[8] which I translated with Nancy Gates Madsen.[9]

Realizing that *The Winter Garden Photograph* was a rich and beautiful collection, I went on to translate the rest of its poems so that the complete book could appear in English. Nancy and I also revised our earlier co-translations for this edition. Otherworldly qualities to poetry by Rodríguez make it oddly challenging to render in English: the poems must feel grounded even as they are escaping us, a balance that Rodríguez strikes in her own idiosyncratic fashion.

In addition to discussing texts with the author, reviewing some of her intertextual sources led me to make specific choices for my new translations in this book. For example, while there is no doubt that her work demonstrates originality, Rodríguez positions herself in dialogue with thinkers and writers with whom she identifies. For this translation I pursued language and imagery suggestive of that dialogue, which meant sometimes drawing on phrases mediated by other writers instead of remaining in a more strict word-for-word translation style.

This expansion is most visible in the title of the book. I had drafted a translation of the title poem with Nancy for the anthology. Our earlier working title for the poem "La foto del invernadero" was "The photo of the greenhouse." This phrasing was correct in a literal sense. However, I was unhappy with it: something was missing, and I didn't know what it was. We left the poem out of our anthology, despite its importance and the vagueness of my dissatisfaction. As I was working on the remainder of the book, I read Barthes's *Camera Lucida* for the

---

8   *Violet Island and Other Poems.* LA: Green Integer, 2004.

9   The twelve poems we co-translated are: "twice is the minimum," "Isle of Wight," "Can I Be God?," "—at least, that's how he looked, backlit—," "the portrait of a young man (Dresden) 1521," "*le couple* (1931)," "dog and boy," "a Thracian rider," "I lost a word," "memory or statue," "a moment of blackness," "the winter garden photograph."

first time. Once I discovered the explicit reference by Rodríguez to Roland Barthes, who discusses his own winter garden photograph, the words of the new translation felt right: richer in sound, and especially in concept.

Throughout *The Winter Garden Photograph*, Rodríguez's composition process and access to non-English sources complicate the question of to what or to whom the English-language translator would be faithful while recreating her poetic registers. For example, Samuel Beckett presents doubly as a source in her book: he originally wrote some of his texts in French, then rewrote them in English as their second incarnation. As a reader of French but not English, Rodríguez might have been exposed at one point to one "original" Beckett but not to its twin, not to the "source" that I was reading in English—or to any other English-language sources and translations that I have referenced. Her Barthes and Woolf, her Sylvia Plath: all were distanced from their incarnations in English.

As a result, fidelity to textual borrowing was an aesthetically useful myth for me, one I used as I worked. Reading these works by the other authors prompted me to change my own uses of English in ways that often made the translations more effective and unexpected as poems. However, "fidelity" does not represent unmediated access to source texts for Rodríguez, or afterwards for me: in other words, there is no simple, precise chain of transmitted vocabulary from writer to writer for the translator to trace. Rather than claiming word-for-word loyalty to the original poems, therefore, I think of the translator's fidelity here as the process of asking how images and concepts from multiple texts may hang together or split apart within the deceptively smooth textures of the poems.

The opportunity to discuss the work with Rodríguez was terrifically valuable to me on this project as an experiment in translation. With her habitual curiosity and open-mindedness, she encouraged me to trespass on her language. One element that we explored together is the reconstruction of her sometimes opaque or personal symbolism.

My "night is falling" is based not only on the original poem's text, but on the poet's memories of past travel through Russia and Europe. Rodríguez told me that the incessant light of the White Nights had kept her up for days before she finally arrived in Madrid, where darkness came like a physical body to meet her. I used this information to make a slight expansion on my version of the poem.

For this edition, Rodríguez took the opportunity to correct errors in the Spanish. We used the edition published in recognition of her second Casa de las Américas prize for poetry (Havana: Fondo Editorial Casa de las Américas, 1998).

This edition includes an interview with Rodríguez conducted by the poet, translator, and scholar Rosa Alcalá in 2001. Their writer-to-writer discussion addresses themes relevant to the poetry in *The Winter Garden Photograph*, as well as many other books by Rodríguez.

The interview took place at a pivotal moment in Rodríguez's evolution as a cultural actor in Havana. Alcalá asks Rodríguez a series of questions related to her foundation of alternative cultural projects in the city. For readers to understand that sense of alternative space, it's important to note that when Cuban leadership expanded the spheres of education and publishing on the island after 1959, it did so under the auspices of the state. In this context, the idea of "alternative" relates to the inevitable tensions that arise around state oversight. A central image is that of bureaucrats as gatekeepers managing artistic support and recognition. This critical image does not represent a blanket rejection of everyone working within state systems, but it serves as an essential structural caution.

In the 1990s Rodríguez became known for opening her rooftop apartment to writers and artists, who gathered there for conversations and events. The informal space at her home therefore became a site not run by a state organization. Alcalá takes this conflation of home/salon as an entry point for their 2001 conversation.

By the time of the interview the rooftop scene had diminished in impact, a subject they discuss directly. To pursue the ideal of artist-run spaces, Rodríguez had now initiated the next step: "Casa de Letras" (a "house" of letters or literature).

Another group in the city soon adopted the same name.[10] Rodríguez then changed the name of her project. We have left "Casa" in this interview because of its historical accuracy.

Considering the space that she was using at the time on top of a palace overlooking Havana's Plaza de Armas, Rodríguez adopted "Torre," or "Tower," in the group's new name. This is the title that endured as her project evolved throughout the first two decades of the twenty-first century, up to the time of this writing. Torre de Letras projects are best designated "semi-independent," in contrast to the prior autonomous salon, because they depend on having a space and other resources authorized by the Cuban Book Institute. Leadership for individual Torre projects is given to writers, the condition that makes them meaningful to Rodríguez.

This reference to towers proved prescient. Cuban authorities closed the palace for renovations, and they moved the Cuban Book Institute into the tallest building on Old Havana's Obispo Street, a renovated bank. Torre de Letras went with it. This landmark building is easy to find, but it turned out to have drawbacks. The room assigned to them for events was far too small. The building's rooftop offers stunning views of the city but, as a result of its height, gets such strong wind that open-air literary events are not realistic. Rodríguez comments that road conditions nearby became a problem too. Even after substantive repairs to the streets around Obispo, she went in search of other options.

During the past decade, events sponsored by Torre de Letras took place in various other locations. Now most happen at the Alma Mater Bookstore. Located at the corner of Infanta and San Lázaro, the store is affiliated with the University of Havana. Torre de Letras offers classes in editing, among other activities.

---

10   On November 30, 2018, Rodríguez sent me emails with the latest updates regarding Casa/Torre projects discussed here.

Torre de Letras also has a tiny publishing wing that promotes new work from Havana as well as newly translated collections from abroad. Poet Ramón Hondal is the current editor, while Yanet Blanco covers the tasks of a managing editor. Editorial decisions are thus still made by a writer. As a parallel philosophy, Rodríguez wants the translations they publish to be rendered by creative writers, in order to produce more effective literary results than what she normally sees from Cuban presses. The Cuban Book Institute continues to supervise and mediate, so actual print production depends on that intercession.

Economic shortfalls at the Institute make the timing of their releases unpredictable. One of their most recent publications is a translation of the 1930 novel *Ferdydurke*, by the Polish author Witold Gombrowicz. The choice recognizes the historic advocacy for the novel in Argentina, including its translation, by exiled Cuban author Virgilio Piñera (1912-1979); the edition was co-sponsored by the publisher Arte y Literatura. Other forthcoming collections include works by Yves Bonnefoy and Pierre Klossowski (both translated by Jorge Miralles) and Hank Lazer (tr. Omar Pérez).

In recent years Rodríguez has relied more on Hondal and Blanco as the local faces of Torre de Letras. She maintains her rooftop apartment on Ánimas Street, and her mother and one of her sons live with other family members in other units of the same building. However, the dispersal of Cuban families into diaspora that now mirrors larger patterns of globalization has affected Rodríguez: her other children live abroad. For reasons I discuss at more length in our edition *Other Letters to Milena / Otras cartas a Milena*, she now spends periods of time in southern Florida. [11]

It's a significant shift. I would still qualify comments suggesting that Rodríguez has left for good (a few of which I have heard during panels at academic conferences) as inaccurate. Home has become

---

11   *Other Letters to Milena / Otras cartas a Milena.* AL: The University of Alabama Press, 2016.

more complex for her, and thanks to her international stature as a writer, international invitations also contribute to the time she spends time abroad. But her real home still centers on a Havana rooftop—or perhaps better said, the idea of home relies on the places where she composed her many past books, among them *The Winter Garden Photograph.*

— Kristin Dykstra, December 2018

The Winter Garden Photograph

… mira —dijeron los mejores de esos peregrinos
que van por el mundo con su Leica— incluso
en ese instante en que has sido ilusión, inconsecuencia,
quizá futilidad, incluso en ese instante
en que no eres nada, en que eres la nada,
eres, y en eso eres todo, eres el todo…

"… see," said the best of those pilgrims who roam
the world, Leica in hand, *"even in that moment
when you are illusion, irrelevance, futility,
even in the instant when you are nothing, when
you are nothingness itself, you are, and, in existing,
you are everything, you are the whole…"*

dos veces son el mínimo

aquí media luz; afuera, la mañana.
miro por la abertura de la media negra
que hace un ángulo exacto con mi pie que está
arriba. un mundo que me interesa
aparece por la cicatriz; un deseo que me interesa
rehusando la prudencia.
los ruidos bajo el sol entrada la mañana.
por la abertura en triángulo del muslo hasta el pie en tu boca
hay un canal.
la total ausencia de intención de este día,
un día en que uno se expone y luego enferma.
un día formando un gran arco entre el dedo que roza
el labio y la media.
dos veces son el mínimo de confianza
para lograr la ilusión. yo, al amanecer,
estaba junto a la ventana (era la única imagen
en la que podría refugiarme) me acercaba para no llegar
y estar convencida —nunca reafirmada—
"como si, para mí, tú, la otra, te abrieras, o te rompieras,
del modo más suave contra el alféizar".
(las palabras siempre son de algún otro, se prestan
para consolar a la sensación que también
viene de allá afuera, incontrolable) otra cosa
es lo que yo hago con ellas aquí adentro:
las caliento escuchando bien un sonido que me revela la tonalidad
de lo que expongo (una ilusión) de ser aquella
que algo vio en el triángulo cuya cúspide es tu boca
absorbiendo también de la sustancia.
yo sólo me aproximaba a la ventana
—escritora nómada— que mira con devoción
en vez de coger a ciegas (la primera vez) sabe que
dos veces son el mínimo de vida de ser.
júrame que no saldremos del "territorio del poema" esta vez
que si estrujo y pierdo en el cesto de los papeles
este cuerpo

twice is the minimum

here half-light; outside, the morning.
I look through the hole of the half-dark stocking
that forms an exact angle with my foot
up there. a world that interests me
appears through the scar; a desire that interests me
refusing prudence.
noise under the mid-morning sun.
through the triangular opening from my thigh to my foot inside
     your mouth
there's a channel.
the complete absence of intention today,
a day to expose oneself and then fall ill.
a day forming a great arc between my stocking and
the toe that grazes a lip.
twice is the minimum for trust
to achieve the illusion. at dawn I
was next to the window (the only image
in which I could hide) I came close but wouldn't arrive
at being convinced—never reaffirmed—
"as if, for me, you, the other woman, opened up, or broke,
in the gentlest way against the windowsill."
(the words always belong to someone else, they lend themselves
to consoling the feeling that also
comes from out there, uncontrollable) something else
is what I do with them here inside:
I warm them listening carefully to a sound that reveals the tonality
of what I expose (an illusion) about being that woman
who saw something, in the triangle with its apex at your mouth,
getting something from the substance as well.
I was just approaching the window
—nomadic writer—who looks on devotedly
instead of grasping blindly (the first time) and knows that
twice is the minimum you can live.
swear to me that we won't leave "the poem's territory" this time
that if I crumple up and lose this body

no voy a renacer al espectáculo. estamos juntos
en el diseño con tinta de un día que no es verdadero
porque osa comprimirse en la línea del encanto.
—de la cintura hacia arriba está la carne, el día.
—de la mitad inferior de tronco (abajo) media negra hasta
la noche, el fin.
júrame que no saldremos de aquí
una casa prestada con ventanas que miran hacia el mar de papel
donde nos desnudamos, rodamos, prestamos palabras para lavar
volver a teñir en el crepúsculo. era mi cuerpo ese
promontorio que tú colocabas al derecho, al revés,
sobre el piso de mármol?
fue esa tumba siempre, los ojillos de los poros
como gusanos olfateando mis pensamientos
para nada?
yo siempre quise ver lo que tú mirabas
por la abertura del triángulo
(ser los dos a la vez) algo doble en el mismo sitio
de los cuerpos y en los pies, longitudes distintas
"para aquel contacto de una suavidad maravillosa".

dos veces son el mínimo de vida de ser.
yo, una vez más, ensayo la posibilidad de renacer
(de la posteridad ya no me inquieta nada).

in the wastebasket
I won't be reborn into the spectacle. we're together
in the inked design of a day that is untrue
because it dares to compress itself in lines of pleasure.
—from the waist up is the flesh, the day.
—from the lower half of the torso (down) the stocking darkens into
the night, the end.
swear to me we won't leave this place
a house on loan with windows opening to the sea of paper
where we undress, roll, lend words to wash
to make more stains in the dusk. was it my body, that
promontory you pointed toward you, then away from you,
on the marble floor?
was it always that tomb, the pores' openings
like worms aimlessly sniffing out
my thoughts?
I always tried to see what you were seeing
through the triangular opening
(to be the two at once) something doubled in the places
for the bodies and the feet, different lengths,
"for that contact of a marvelous gentleness."

twice is the minimum you can live.
I test the possibility of rebirth one more time
(nothing about posterity worries me anymore).

la isla de Wight

yo era como aquella chica de la isla de Wight
—el poema no estaba terminado
era el centro del poema lo que nunca estaba terminado—
ella había buscado
desesperadamente
ese indicio de la arboladura.
había buscado...
hasta no tener respuestas ni preguntas
y ser lo mismo que cualquiera
bajo esa indiferencia de la materia
a su necesidad. el yo se agrieta.
(un yo criminal y lúdico que la abraza
a través de los pastos ocres y resecos del verano)
ella había buscado "la infinitud azul del universo en el ser".
—lo que dicen gira en torno a sus primeros años
cuando el padre murió sin haber tenido demasiado
conocimiento del poema—.
sé que esa mentira que ha buscado
obtiene algún sentido al derretirse
en sus ojos oscuros. ha buscado el abrupto sentido del sentir
que la rodea.
(un poema es lo justo, lo exacto, lo irrepetible,
dentro del caos que uno intenta ordenar y ser)
y lo ha ordenado para que el poema no sea necesario.
despojada del poema y de mí
va buscando con su pasión de perseguir
la dualidad. ha perdido, ha buscado.
ha contrapuesto animales antagónicos que han venido a morir
bajo mi aparente neutralidad de especie,
un gato, un pez, un pájaro... sólo provocaciones.
—te digo que los mires—
para hallar otra cosa entre esa línea demoledora de las formas
que chocan al sentir su resonancia.
—también aquí se trata del paso del tiempo,
de la travesía del mar por el poema—

Isle of Wight

I was like that girl from the Isle of Wight
—the poem wasn't finished
it was the center of the poem that was never finished
she had searched
desperately
for some sign of its rigging.
she had searched…
until she had neither answers nor questions
and was the same as anyone else
under matter's indifference
to her need. the I cracks.
(a criminal and ludic I who embraces her
through dry, ochre, summer grasses)
she had searched for "the universe's blue infinity in the self."
—what they say revolves around her early years
when her father died without knowing too much
about the poem.
I know that the lie she's been looking for
gathers meaning when it melts
inside her dark eyes. she has looked for the abrupt sense of sensing
that surrounds her.
(a poem is the precise thing, the accurate thing, the unrepeatable thing
within the chaos that one tries to arrange and become)
and she has arranged it so the poem won't be necessary.
stripped of the poem and of me
she goes on looking with her passion for pursuing
duality. she has lost, she has searched.
she has counterposed antagonistic animals that have come to die
under my apparent neutrality with regard to species
a cat, a fish, a bird… only provocations.
—I'm telling you to look at them—
to find something else in that devastating line of shapes
that collide as they sense their resonance.
here too it deals with the passage of time,
with the ocean traveling through the poem—

adonde ellos iban, los poemas no habían llegado todavía.
yo era como aquella chica de la isla de Wight
había buscado en lo advenedizo
la fuga y la permanencia de lo fijo y me hallo
dispuesta a compartir con ella a través de las tachaduras
si el poema había existido alguna vez materialmente
si había sido escrito ese papel
para conservar el lugar de una espera.

wherever they were going, the poems hadn't yet arrived.
I was like that girl from the Isle of Wight
I had searched foreignness
for escape and the permanence of definition and I find myself
disposed to let her know through the crossed-out words
whether the poem had existed materially at any time
whether that paper had been written
to preserve a place for waiting.

can I be God?

para Silvia Plath

Cada día es una plegaria renovada para que dios
exista para que me visite con mayor fuerza y claridad.

—Silvia Plath

la amiga de Alicia, una amiga mía, vivió en Inglaterra.
—la amiga de mi amiga Alicia, no la del cuento—
conoció a un hombre que hacía pastar su rebaño
cerca de la cabaña donde Silvia y Ted
habían tenido a su segundo hijo. ella lo invitó a un trago
—muy eufórica—
y el hombre que no sabía nada de poesía
sólo recordaba que Silvia era
una mujer que caminaba sola por los páramos
al atardecer.
no conozco a la amiga de mi amiga,
pero alargando ese final
encuentro una nota con su foto —al fondo—
y le agradezco ese trago de vino donde
echó sus palabras hacia el atardecer,
que además de traernos el mes de abril
las islitas de sílabas con un poco de color
donde sobresalen preguntas sin respuestas a Dios
(*Dear God, can I be God?*)
vuelven a mirar la sonrisa pendiente
de un milagro. la blanca espuma de la leche
para que se enfríe
junto al sol naranja de sus ojos prendidos en el horno,
Silvia y Ted tenían una casita
en el atardecer de los páramos
cubierta por plantas tupidas y tallos muy altos
donde uno (a la luz del atardecer
cree que todo es posible;

can I be God?

for Sylvia Plath

> Every day is a renewed prayer that the god exists, that he
> will visit with increased force and clarity.
>
> —Sylvia Plath

Alice's friend, a friend of mine, lived in England.
my friend Alice—not Alice from the story—her friend
met a man who sent his flock to graze
near the cabin where Sylvia and Ted
had their second child. she invited him over for a drink
—euphoric—
and the man who knew nothing about poetry
only remembered that Sylvia was
a woman who walked alone across the moors
at sundown.
I don't know my friend's friend,
but extending that ending
I find a note on the bottom of her photo
and I thank her for the glass of wine in which
she threw her words at the setting sun,
bringing us the month of April
with a touch of color
where unanswered questions for God appear
(*Dear God, can I be God?*)
and little syllabic islands form the remarkable smile
of a miracle. milk's white foam
grows cold by the orange light of her eyes, glowing from the oven.
Sylvia and Ted had a little house
in the sunset on the moors
covered by thick plants and tall stalks
where she (in the dusky light)
believed that everything was possible,
even becoming God.

incluso convertirse in Dios).
ella se levantaba muy temprano
y vomitaba con horror su imposibilidad
—la retama roja y amarilla—
dentro de una palabra de cristal
que pujaba y pujaba sin poder jamás
convertirse en él,
(una afirmación como un latigazo. Dios).
era una niña desaliñada
que conoció a la Sra. Davies
y a la Sra. Plum y al comandante Crump,
pero que no podía convertirse en Dios
pero que podía creer en él
pero que no podía saltar sobre su otra religión
y caer al abismo
sin artificialidad alguna.
y el hombre que en tiempos de Plath
hacía pacer su rebaño cerca de la cabaña
lo concentró todo en el cuenco de vino
en la espuma de leche
en el fuego naranja del zorro que sabía,
cómo abandonaría el cuerpo de la muchacha
exactamente a la hora especificada
porque, aunque la paciente parecía poseída,
su mal no era posesión, sino la emoción
del remordimiento por no poder convertirse en Dios
(ni a Ted, ni a su padre, ni a su madre, ni a sus amigos, en Dios).
y así perdió el sentido de su individualidad
hacia el atardecer, de un morado increíblemente
intenso como el vino
en la casita, que no era una cabaña sino un templo
para su crucifixión
donde la amiga de mi amiga Alicia —no la del cuento—
la vio a través de los ojos de Dios
la última vez.

she used to rise very early
and regurgitate her impossibility with horror
—red and yellow furze—
in a crystal word
that struggled and struggled without ever
transforming into him
(statement like a whiplash. God).
she was a slovenly girl
who met Mrs. Davies
and Mrs. Plum and Major Crump,
but who couldn't change into God
but who could believe in him
but who couldn't leap over her other religion
and fall into the abyss
without any artificiality.
and the man who in Plath's times
sent his flock to graze near the cabin
concentrated everything on the tumbler of wine,
on the milk's foam,
on the orange flame of the fox who knew
how he would abandon the girl's body
exactly at the specified hour
because, though the patient seemed possessed,
her evil was not possession but the emotion
of guilt for being incapable of transforming into God
(or transforming Ted, or her father, or her mother, or her friends,
    into God).
and so she lost herself
toward nightfall, a purple incredibly
intense like wine
in the little house, which was not a cabin but a temple
for her crucifixion
where my friend Alice's friend—not Alice from the story—
saw her through the eyes of God
the last time.

—al menos, así lo veía a contra luz—

para Fernando García

he prendido sobre la foto una tachuela roja.
—sobre la foto famosa y legendaria—
el ectoplasma de lo que ha sido,
lo que se ve en el papel es tan seguro
como lo que se toca. la fotografía
tiene algo que ver con la resurrección.
—quizás ya estaba allí
en lo real en el pasado
con aquel que veo ahora en el retrato.
los bizantinos decían que la imagen de Cristo
en el sudario de Turín no estaba hecha
por la mano del hombre.
he deportado ese real hacia el pasado;
he prendido sobre la foto una tachuela roja.
a través de esa imagen (en la pared, en la foto)
somos otra vez contemporáneos.
la reserva del cuerpo en el aire de un rostro,
esa anímula, tal como él mismo,
aquel a quien veo ahora en el retrato
algo moral, algo frío.

era a finales de siglo y no había escapatoria.
la cúpula había caído, la utopía
de una bóveda inmensa sujeta a mi cabeza,
había caído.
el Cristo negro de la Iglesia del Cristo
—al menos, así lo veía a contra luz—
reflejando su alma en pleno mediodía.
podía aún fotografiar al Cristo aquel;
tener esa resignación casual
para recuperar la fe.
también volver los ojos para mirar las hojas amarillas,

—at least, that's how he looked, backlit—

for Fernando García

I stuck a red tack into the photo.
—into the famous, legendary photo—
the ectoplasm of what has been,
what you see on the paper is as secure
as what you touch. photography
has something to do with resurrection.
—maybe he was already there
in what was real, in the past
with the distant man whom I now see in the portrait.
the Byzantines said that Christ's image
on the shroud of Turin wasn't made
by the hand of man.
I've exiled that reality into the past;
I stuck a red tack into the photo.
through that image (on the wall, in the photo)
we're contemporaries again.
the body's reserve in a face's demeanor,
that speck of life, like the man himself,
that distant man whom I now see in the photo
somewhat moral, somewhat cold.

it was the end of a century and there was no way out.
the dome had fallen, the utopia,
an immense vault billowing from my head,
had fallen.
the black Christ from the Church of Christ
—at least, that's how he looked, backlit—
reflecting his soul at high noon.
I could still photograph that distant Christ;
could have the casual resignation
to recover my faith.
could look again, too, at the yellow leaves,

el fantasma de árbol del Parque Central,
su fuente seca.
(y tú que me exiges todavía alguna fe.)

mi amigo era el hijo supuesto o real.
traía los poemas en el bolsillo
del pantalón escolar.
siempre fue un muchacho poco común
al que no pude amar
porque tal vez, lo amé. la madre (su madre),
fue su amante (mental?)
y es a lo que más le temen.
qué importa si alguna vez se conocieron
en un plano más real.
en la casa frente al Malecón, tenía aquel
viejo libro de Neruda dedicado por él.
no conozco su letra, ni tampoco la certeza.
no sé si algo pueda volver a ser real.
su hijo era mi amigo,
entre la curva azul y amarilla del mar.
lo que se ve en el papel es tan seguro
como lo que se toca. (aprieto la tachuela roja,
el clic del disparador... lo que se ve no es
la llama de la pólvora, sino el minúsculo relámpago
de una foto).
el hijo, (su hijo) vive en una casa amarilla
frente al Malecón —nadie lo sabe, él tampoco lo sabe—
es poeta y carpintero.
desde niño le ponían una boina
para que nadie le robara la ilusión de ser,
algún día, como él.
algo en la cuenca del ojo, cierta irritación;
algo en el silencio y en la voluntad
se le parece. entre la curva azul
y amarilla del mar.
—dicen que aparecieron en la llanura
y que no estaba hecha por la mano del hombre—
quizás ya estaba allí, esperándonos.
la verosimilitud de la existencia es lo que importa,

at the ghost of a tree in Havana's Central Park,
its fountain dry.
(and you who still require faith from me.)

my friend was the supposed or real son.
he carried poems in the pocket
of his school uniform.
he was always an unusual boy,
one I couldn't love,
maybe because I loved him already. the mother (his mother)
was his (mental?) lover
and she is what they fear the most in him.
what does it matter if they once met each other
on a more real level.
in the house on the Malecón, he had that
old book by Neruda, dedicated.
I'm not familiar with his handwriting—or certainty, either.
I don't know if anything can be real again.
his son was my friend,
between the blue and yellow curves of the sea.
what you see on the paper is as secure
as what you touch. (I press down on the red tack,
the click of the shutter… what you see isn't
the flash of gunpowder, but the tiny lightning
of a photo.)
the son (his son) lives in a yellow house
on the Malecón—no one knows it, he doesn't know it either—
he's a poet and a carpenter.
they've made him wear a beret since he was a child
so no one could steal his illusion that he would be,
someday, like his father.
something in the eye socket, a certain irritation;
something in the silence and in the resolve
seems like him. between the blue and yellow
curves of the sea.
—it's said they appeared on the plain
and the image wasn't made by the hand of man—
maybe he was already there, waiting for us.
the verisimilitude of existence is what matters,

pura arqueología de la foto, de la razón.
(y tú que me exiges todavía alguna fe)

el Cristo negro de la Isla del Cristo sigue intocable,
a pesar de la falsificación que han hecho
de su carne en la restauración;
la amante sigue intocable
y asiste a los homenajes en los aniversarios;
(su hijo), mi amigo, el poeta, el carpintero de Malecón,
pisa con sus sandalias cuarteadas
las calles de La Habana;
los bares donde venden un ron barato a granel
y vive en una casa amarilla
entre la curva azul y oscurecida del mar.
qué importancia tiene haber vivido
por más de quince años tan cerca del espíritu de aquel,
de su rasgo más puro, de su ilusión genética,
debajo de la sombra corrompida
del árbol único del verano treinta años después?
si él ha muerto, si él también va a morir?

no me atrevo a poner la foto legendaria sobre la pared.
un simple clic del disparador, una tachuela roja
y los granos de plata que germinan
        (su inmortalidad)
anuncian que la foto también ha sido atacada
por la luz; que la foto también morirá
por la humedad del mar, la duración;
el contacto, la devoción, la obsesión
fatal de repetir tantas veces que seríamos como él.
en fin, por el miedo a la resurrección,
porque a la resurrección toca también la muerte.

sólo me queda saber que se fue, que se es
la amante imaginaria de un hombre imaginario
        (laberíntico)
la amiga real del poeta de Malecón,
con el deseo insuficiente del ojo que captó
su muerte literal, fotografiando cosas

the pure archeology of the photo, of reason.
(and you who still require faith from me.)

the black Christ from the Island of Christ is still untouchable,
in spite of the forgery they've made
of his flesh in the restoration;
the lover is still untouchable
and attends homages on anniversaries;
(his son) my friend, the poet, the carpenter of the Malecón,
walks in cracked sandals through
the streets of Havana,
through bars where cheap rum overflows,
and lives in a yellow house
between the blue and darkened curves of the sea.
what does it matter to have lived
for more than fifteen years so close to the spirit of that distant man,
to his purest feature, to his genetic illusion,
under the corrupted shadow
of the summer's only tree, thirty years later?
if he has died, if he too will die?

I don't dare put the legendary photo on the wall.
a simple click of the shutter, a red tack
and the germinating grains of silver
        (his immortality)
announce that the photo has also been attacked
by the light; that the photo will also die
from the ocean's dampness, its duration;
the contact, the devotion, the fatal
obsession of repeating so many times that we would be like him.
anyway, for fear of resurrection,
because resurrection too is touched by death.

the only thing left for me is to know that I was, that I am
the imaginary lover of an imaginary man
        (labyrinthine)
the real friend of the poet of the Malecón,
with the same insufficient desire as the eye that captured
his literal death, photographing things

para ahuyentarlas del espíritu después;
al encontrarse allí, en lo real en el pasado
en lo que ha sido
por haber sido hecha para ser como él;
en la muerte real de un pasado imaginario
—en la muerte imaginaria de un pasado real—
donde no existe esta fábula, ni la importancia
o la impotencia de esta fábula,
sin el derecho a develarla
(un poema nos da el derecho a ser ilegítimos en algo más
que su trascendencia y su corruptibilidad).
un simple clic del disparador
y la historia regresa como una protesta de amor
        (Michelet)
pero vacía y seca. como la fuente del Parque Central
o el fantasma de hojas caídas que fuera su árbol protector.
ha sido atrapada por la luz (la historia, la verdad)
la que fue o quiso ser como él,
la amistad del que será no será jamás su hijo,
la mujer que lo amó desde su casa abierta,
anónima, en la página cerrada de Malecón;
debajo de la sombra del clic del disparador
abierto muchas veces
en los ojos insistentes del muchacho
cuya almendra oscurecida
aprendió a mirar
y a callar
como elegido.
(y tú me exiges todavía alguna fe?)

in order to drive them away from the spirit afterwards;
finding myself there, in what was real, in the past,
in what has been,
by having been made in order to be like him;
in the real death of an imaginary past
—in the imaginary death of a real past—
where this fable doesn't exist, or the importance
or the impotence of this fable,
without the right to unveil it
(a poem gives us the right to be illegitimate in something more
than its transcendence and its corruptibility).
a simple click of the shutter
and history returns like a declaration of love
        (Michelet)
but empty and dry. like the fountain in Central Park
or the leafless ghost that once was a protective tree.
she has been trapped by light (history, truth),
the woman who was or who wanted to be like him,
the friendship with the one who will be, who will never be his son,
the woman who loved him from her open house,
anonymous, on the closed page of the Malecón;
under the shadow of the shutter's click
opened many times
in the boy's insistent eyes,
darkened almonds that
learned to see
and to be silent
as if chosen.
(and you still require some faith from me?)

los días

los días afuera, con esa luz que
baja hasta perder su definición
y no saber si la luz sale de mí (adentro)
me bebe hacia sus claros horizontes, o está pintada
al borde del muro para continuar
el enceguecimiento de su propia claridad.
yo extraño la canción que de mi boca recorría
el tiempo inmenso en cada sílaba de su penetración.
eso era ser joven. cuando aún, verde y tibia
masticaba las ramitas de toronja con indiferencia.
lívida, hoy cruzo este discurso de los días
que ya no pueden sorprenderme
—con su arete pequeño de plata en el lóbulo izquierdo—
bestia y muchacho, para recorrer el resultado feroz de los días,
su alucinación de oscurecer sin morir en la carrera
hacia la perdición.
un azoro en la nuca
y ser el rostro efímero de cualquiera
(de la mujer del disco, por ejemplo) que se raya
al volver desde tus manos grandes.
un rostro, que sobreimpuesto al mío,
es un rostro encarnizado en morir bajo la misma luz
donde ella y yo hemos permanecido
en lo curvado
en lo que se ha hecho grieta al roer de los días
en lo que ya no te pertenece
en lo que ya no es mi juventud
y todo queda amenazado por la curva
que la trajo y me regresa.

the days

the days outside, their light that
sinks until it loses definition—
not knowing whether the light emanates from me (within),
if it drinks me towards its pale horizons, or if it's painted
out toward the edge of the wall, still spreading
the blindingness of its clarity.
I miss the song that used to come from my mouth,
the immensity of time in every penetrating syllable.
that was youth. still green, generating warmth,
I chewed grapefruit branches indifferently.
today I pale across this discourse about the days
that can't surprise me anymore
—a small silver earring in his left lobe—
beast and boy, moving through the terrible outcome of the days,
his hallucination of darkening, but not dying, on the road
to loss.
quiver along the nape of the neck
—being the ephemeral face of any woman
(the woman on the record, for example) all scratched up,
returning from your expansive hands.
a face, superimposed on mine,
a face forcefully incarnate in death under the same light
where she and I have remained motionless
inside something curved
inside a crack made by the scraping days
inside what doesn't belong to you any more
inside what isn't my youth any more
and everything is still threatened by the curve
that brought her and sends me back.

el frío

el frío fuerte pasó
y los días de marzo han vuelto
con su polvo del sur a levantar la hojarasca.
días para quedarse a vivir eternamente en el vaivén;
días en que nada más que una calma
de mediodía común estremece algún vidrio.
si me estuviera permitido
quedarme en esa falla del tiempo,
sólo para recibir su luna nueva y no pasar
—tampoco detenerme— sentarme allí en el
tiovivo a revivir su pausa
que golpea y endulza mi piel
como un arquero ciego.
y pensar que se puede volver a uno como un niño!
si el espíritu se decide por el regreso a sí mismo
un poco atolondrado después de haber salido
del exceso de alegría y de pena;
nunca seguros ante el sinsentido de este día
que no pretende la inteligencia ni la razón
que no permite que tu belleza
envejezca en los desgastes terrenales
y te hace mirar al cielo por la estrecha pausa
que su serenidad ha impuesto.
a ti, recién llegado de cualquier fortuna
contra el éxtasis de estar aquí, conmigo en este día,
te pido que vuelvas más tarde.
poco después, cuando empieza a oscurecer
su resplandor, la noche.

the cold

the bitter cold ended
and the days of March returned.
their southern dust rises with storming leaves.
days for staying to live eternity inside the oscillation;
days in which nothing more than inactivity
rattles some windowpane at ordinary noontime.
if I were permitted
to stay here, inside this fault line in time,
just to receive its new moon and not to move on
—not to stay—to sit down there on the
merry-go-round and revive its pause
that thumps against my skin and softens it
like a blind archer.
and to think that you can come back to yourself as a child!
if the spirit chooses to return to itself,
a little disoriented after exiting
the excess of happiness and pain;
we're never safe from the meaninglessness of this day
that doesn't claim intelligence or reason
that doesn't allow your beauty
to age with earthly wear and tear
and forces you to look up at the sky through the walled-in pause
imposed by its serenity.
as for you, recently arrived through whatever destiny runs
counter to the ecstasy of being here, with me, in this day,
I ask you to come back later.
a little later, when the day's splendor begins
to dim with night.

la diferencia

yo que he visto la diferencia,
en la sombra que aún proyectan los objetos en mis ojos
—esa pasión de reconstruir la pérdida;
el despilfarro de la sensación—
del único país que no es lejano
a donde vas. donde te quedas.
sé que en la tablilla de terracota
que data del reinado de algún rey,
con caligrafía japonesa en forma de surcos
están marcados tus días.
los días son el lugar donde vivimos
no hay otro espacio que la franja que traspasan
tus ojos al crepúsculo.
no podrás escoger otro lugar que
el sitio de los días,
su diferencia.
y en esa rajadura entre dos mundos
renacer a una especie (más estética)
donde podamos vivir otra conciencia de los días
sin los despilfarros de cada conquista.

the difference

I, who have seen the difference
in shadow cast by objects across my eyes
—the passion for reconstructing loss;
the extravagance of sensation—
in the only country that isn't far away
where you go. where you stay.
I know your days are recorded
on the terracotta tablet
—dating from the reign of some king or another—
in wrinkles of Japanese calligraphy.
the days are the place where we live
there's no space other than a strip over which your eyes
pass at sunset.
you won't be able to choose any place other than
the location of the days,
their difference.
and in that crack between two worlds
to be reborn into a (more aesthetic) species
where we could live a different awareness of the days
without the extravagances of each conquest.

cámara secreta

dentro de un cofrecito de ébano
junto a la cama mortuoria de Tutankamen yacen
los fabulosos tesoros del joven rey en el Nilo.
allí encontré una pieza dorada
como una muñeca, o una antigua miniatura india.
alguien me permitió abrir y quizás ver
aquel secreto que soñaba
(en cada sueño perdemos evidentemente
una inocencia) soy otra vez Pigmalión
siempre a la espera de cualquier milagro.
si uno va todo el camino junto a las cosas,
uno puede cubrir todo el camino de ficciones
y ciertamente uno recibe su recompensa
siempre completamente diferente
a la esperada. si alguien,
al menos durmiera sin estar muerto
junto al cofre de un rey
y recibiera un sueño como el mío,
—la miniatura de cristal de Atlántida—
entraríamos de una vez en la inocencia.

12 de agosto de 1995

secret chamber

inside a small ebony coffer
next to the deathbed of Tutankhamun lie
the fabulous treasures of the young king of the Nile.
I found a piece there, golden
as a doll, or an ancient Indian miniature.
someone let me open up and try to peer inside
the secret being dreamed
(in each dream we evidently lose
a kind of innocence) I'm Pygmalion again
always waiting for a miracle.
if you walk the length of the road next to your possessions,
you can pave its entirety with fictions
and certainly you receive your recompense,
always completely different
than the one you expected. if anyone
could sleep, deathless,
next to the coffer of a king
and receive a dream like mine
—crystalline miniature from Atlantis—
we would enter innocence in a single stroke.

August 12, 1995

el retrato de un hombre joven (Dresde) 1521

sentado sobre un bloque de madera
ante un fondo caliente, rojo
está ebrio o está dormido
mientras yo trazo un círculo en el punto
de intersección con el eje central que constituye su ombligo
—igual que para el pecho o la cadera estrecha—
que traza también un eje con su pelvis y mi mano.
tengo un modelo señor
el tono claro de sus manos y la carta a punto de caer atraen mi mirada
la luminosa claridad de la camisa, el rostro
como una cúpula sobre la pirámide del tronco
que, dentro de una estructura formada por diagonales
me hace sentir su frialdad, las raras líneas
que le conceden una presencia inmediata
pero no es verdad. la cabeza que está modelada de adentro
hacia afuera donde resalta el retrato de un joven en madera
siguió en la galería de los Viejos Maestros.
su composición es sencillamente clásica
sólo el blanco luminoso hasta el negro de las botas
llena este cuadro de vida. tenemos ante nosotros a un joven
—que no es Durero— él ya se ha ido. y que consciente de
    sí mismo, yace
(pluma y pincel sobre fondo verde blanqueado y lavado).

6 de junio de 1995

the portrait of a young man (Dresden) 1521

seated on a wooden block
in front of a vibrant red backdrop
he's drunk or he's asleep
as I trace a circle at the point
of intersection with the central axis, his navel
—same for his chest, or his narrow hip—
which traces another axis with his pelvis and my hand.
Lord, I have a model
the pale shade of his hands and the letter about to fall capture my eye
the brilliant clarity of the shirt, the face
like a cupola topping the torso's pyramid,
communicating his chill, through its structure
of diagonals, the peculiar lines
that grant him presence, immediate
but unreal. the head is modeled from within
to without, where the portrait of a young man, oil on panel,
is displayed. it was still in the Old Masters' gallery.
the composition is classically simple.
only the brilliant white descending to the black of his boots
fills this painting with life. we have in front of us a young man
—who isn't Dürer: he's gone now. self-aware, this man rests
(pen and paintbrush on a cloudy green, washed background).

June 6, 1995

le couple (1931)

un escultor francés de origen ruso,
esculpió tu rostro en el yeso
(escogió este instante y no otro; escogió este cuadro,
o ninguno) el triángulo del mentón, el gesto
que se inclina para ofrecer la boca
el alcohol almacenado en las venas del cuello
azules blancas ácidas
el deseo, el ángulo de la clavícula al ojo
una fortificación (un puente) al beso.
delante, hacia la izquierda de la sombra de mi rostro, vaga
—el fondo siempre es negro—
el relieve de tu belleza, la oquedad de mis ojos
(yo observaba las sombras, luego descubrí que esas sombras
poseían luz, o cierto resplandor que hería si no inclinaba
los párpados para verte)
quedamos eternamente allí, en la pareja de Ossip Zadkine
un escultor francés de origen ruso
que no nos conoció.

le couple (1931)

a French sculptor of Russian origin
modeled your face in plaster
(he chose this instant and no other; he chose this scene,
or none at all) the triangle of your chin, the gesture
of bending to offer your mouth,
the alcohol stored in the veins of your neck
blue white acid ones
desire, the angle between the collarbone and eye
a fortification (a bridge) to the kiss.
foregrounded to the left of the shadow from my face
—the background is always black—
your beauty wanders in relief, and the hollowness of my eyes
(I looked closely at the shadows, then I discovered that they
held light, or a certain gleam that would be blinding if I didn't lower
my eyelids to see you),
we stay there, eternally in Ossip Zadkine's pairing
a French sculptor of Russian origin
who never met us.

perro y muchacho

escuché el canto de la agonía de los gatos
hacia la puesta del sol. dos gatos hembras
amenazados por sus ladridos y el muchacho
—que con su palo jugaba a ordenar el sinsentido de la tarde.
el sonido agudo del miedo me paralizó
venía de otras regiones del conocimiento,
de lugares donde no existe la posesión, o del
desamparo de la pasión de sus garras.
—una amarilla; la otra, negra—
el aullido me hizo mirar hacia aquella región
en donde vives, oh Dios, oh naturaleza, oh mente!
que me has distanciado de ti
para unirme sólo después, en el gesto de extenderme en la distancia
de esta sangre que se enfría y miente
cuando más inflamable que nunca puede sentir
que es en ti, no en la diferencia contigo,
donde se encuentra aquel a quien rodeas y matas
para hacerlo tuyo.

escuché y luego, ya no oí más,
el canto de la agonía de los gatos
hacia la puesta del sol.

dog and boy

I listened to the cats' agonized chorus
for the setting sun. two females
threatened by the barking and the boy
who arranged the evening's meaninglessness with a stick.
the acute sound of fear paralyzed me.
it came from other regions of knowledge,
from places where possession doesn't exist, or from
their claws' neglected passion.
—one yellow cat; the other, black—
the wailing drew my attention toward the area
where you live, ah God, nature, mind!
—you've distanced yourself from me
to join me only later, in the gesture of spreading me into the distance,
in this blood that cools and dissimulates
when, more inflammable than ever, it can sense
not its difference from you, but the place inside you
where you find that distant man whom you encircle and kill
to make him yours.

I listened, then no longer heard,
the cats' agonized chorus
for the setting sun.

un caballero tracio

un caballero tracio del siglo II me contempla
desde el relieve votivo
donde alguien lo petrificó
sobre el caballo. Oh Plutonio! condenado eternamente
yo digo el salmo de tu destino cercano, yo toco
los arabescos carcomidos y espoleados al sol en su venganza.
(la sierpe observa a la derecha cualquier movimiento
para saltar si te equivocas y enroscarte)
pero sólo asusta a los insectos que mordisquean
las frutas que el caballo reventó contra el fango.
ha pasado un segundo antes de tu muerte
y la sonrisa de bronce y plomo
deja un sabor ocre en mis labios. te he besado
contra el papel moderno de la fotografía
y nos hemos confundido en ese instante
donde me quedo en ti
donde vienes con tu destino cercano tras un rostro antiguo
y yo hago la escritura de mi boca en la piedra.
de dónde provienen tantas cosas que antes fuimos
aquí-ahora?

a Thracian rider

a Thracian rider from the second century watches me
from the votive relief
where someone turned him to stone
on top of his horse. Plutonius! eternally condemned
I recite the psalm of your approaching destiny, I touch
the arabesques, worm-eaten and spurred toward the sun in vengeance.
(from the right the serpent watches for any movement
ready to jump out if you make a mistake and coil around you)
but it only frightens the insects nibbling on
fruit that the horse breaks into the mud.
it happened an instant before your death
and the bronzed and leaden smile
leaves an ochre taste on my lips. I kissed you
on your modern photo paper
and we blurred in that instant
where I remain in you
where you come with your approaching destiny behind an ancient face
and I trace my mouth's writing on rock.
where do they come from, so many things that we once were,
here-now?

posesión

no confirmo haber regresado, o haber estado allí.
mi viaje mental puede ser
la posesión de un recuerdo que ha insistido
sobre mí. (siempre estuve en los ojos del gato
y sé que él me miraba. reflejada,
no he podido moverme de los ojos del gato).
engaños son esos misterios del tiempo
degradándome a una memoria comprendida.
ahora sé que estoy aquí, frente a las luces
del árbol. he comprobado la diferencia en los objetos
y ellos pretenden también engañarme.
en una reproducción de mi necesidad de estar anclada.
en ti, en ellos.
me encojo esta noche de lluvia,
y no confirmo nada.
me importa la fijeza, el bordado de esa pequeña rama
en la hoja más verde.
porque el mundo cabe en los ojos del gato,
de un gato, de ese gato,
que al olerme determina mi lugar.

possession

I don't confirm having come back. or having been there.
my mental travel can mean
taking possession of a memory that persistently
screened me. (I was always inside the cat's eyes
and I know he was looking at me. a reflection,
I can't get out of the cat's eyes.)
those mysteries of time are deceptions.
they degrade me to an apprehended memory.
now I know I'm here, by the lights on
the tree. I've verified the otherness in objects
and they try to deceive me back.
reproducing my need to be anchored.
in you, in them.
I shrink on this rainy night and
confirm nothing.
steadiness matters to me, the embroidery of the little branch
on the greenest leaf.
because the world fits into the eyes of the cat,
of a cat, of that cat,
who sniffing determines my location.

otoño en el pisapapel

su hijo (un hijo) trae un olor a leche agria
que embelesa mientras se disuelve
lo blanco (pan y leche) en el centro
y el coro alza la voz en el templo de Notre Dame
corre entre los árboles con el otoño
amarillo fugaz de la sangre que se espesa
(miel y vino) paisaje que se ha congelado
en espera del grito del niño
que nacerá cuando regrese de parirlo otra vez,
en el gesto de esa mano que alcanza su ansiedad
—de la ilusión del nacimiento contra las pérdidas
de cada corazón en el frío. hay gotas
muy finas de agua helada en mis pestañas
—locura, llanto— fantasía de cristal en el árbol;
kilómetro cero donde se encuentran
las carreteras de Francia (geografía del niño que nació
en el nudo del hielo) tú estás aquí conmigo,
para que se ilumine
la creencia en el cielo…
y tu hijo viene contigo del brazo de la crucifixión
(un hijo) en el vientre de otra, en el vientre
del pisapapel
al voltear la cabeza y la nieve dentro del cristal
frente a la iglesia, en mi vientre,
dentro de unos ojos castaños (sus ojos)
que miran los míos
y el coro alza su voz en el templo de Notre Dame
—yo tiemblo— por tu hijo, por mi vientre,
que parirá siempre de algún encuentro equívoco
al pisar otra vez el círculo de los caminos,
el círculo para resistir
un domingo cualquiera,
tanta belleza
en el centro de cada ciudad.

autumn inside the paperweight

her son (a son) smells of sour milk
bewitching as the whiteness
dissolves (bread and milk) at the center
and the chorus lifts its voice in the temple at Notre Dame
running among autumnal trees
their transient yellow of blood thickening through
the (honey and wine) landscape that has frozen
as it waited for the cry of the child
who will be born when she gets back from giving birth again,
in the gesture of a hand that catches at anxiety
—about the illusion of birth battling every heart's losses
in the cold. there are fine
droplets of water frozen to my eyelashes
—madness, wailing— fantasy glinting in a tree;
kilometer zero where the highways
of France come together (geography of the son born
at the icy junction) you are here with me,
so belief might be
illumined across the sky…
and your son arrives in your arms from the crucifixion
(a son) inside another woman's womb, inside the womb
of a paperweight
head and snow revolving under its glass
in front of a church, inside my womb,
inside some brown eyes (his eyes)
that look into mine
and the chorus lifts its voice in the temple at Notre Dame
—I shiver— for your son, for my womb
which will always give birth after some equivocal encounter
when I walk the circle of the roads again,
the circle for resisting
the same old Sundays,
so much beauty
at the center of every city.

y en la abadía

en la abadía hay un lago
en el lago una cruz de agua
   (otra de madera)
y el Cristo que se refleja allí está
carcomido.
su otra mitad falta.
donde estuvo la pierna ya no hay
quien la cubra
con una manta azul. el Cristo
estrecho de la abadía de Royaumont
me ha mirado y yo lo quiero abrazar
paladeando el pan que ha entrado
en mi boca con el otoño.
(pisar ese canal donde se refleja
en el paisaje de otro siglo, otro lugar,
bajo la suerte de estar aquí
hecha carne otra vez
con el sabor del pan
mojado y frío entre mis labios).
para volver
salvada de la profesión de mí
salvada de los poderes que corrompen
la madera
—cuando se hunde el corcho en la copa
y transpiro— Dios sabe qué,
nace de la cruz doble en el espacio de mi dedo
y él está húmedo y oscuro
en el nicho
esperándome.

and in the abbey

in the abbey there's a lake
in the lake, a cross of water
   (another of wood)
and the Christ reflected there is
corroded.
his other half is missing.
where the leg was there's
no one to cover it
with blue cloth. slender
Christ in the abbey at Royaumont
gazes at me and I want to embrace him
savoring bread that enters
my mouth with autumn.
(to step into the channel where his reflection appears
inside the landscape of another century, another place,
subject to the fate of being here
made flesh once more
tasting wet, cold
bread between my lips.)
to return
saved from self-profession
saved from the powers that corrupt
the wood
—when the cork sinks in the cup
and I sweat out—God knows what,
born out of the double cross the size of my finger
and he is wet and dark
inside the niche
waiting for me.

todo arena

paisaje bajo la luna
del brazo de un hombre que se arrodilla
frente a la iglesia abandonada
oscuridad
al inicio de los callejones;
un aro de agua que brota de un manantial
imaginado
teatro de arena cuyos frontis coronan
gabletes ya destruidos del tiempo
de los Tudores;
la terminal vacía
donde recojo estas piedras que acaricio
para hacerlas perfectas
y mi hombro
equidistante a los rieles
que saldrán después
de un paisaje que gana o pierde fuerza
nos mata o nos revive en su deriva
ya sea en la superficie del papel
donde me escondo,
en la iglesia abandonada
o en el Levante, todo arena.

everything sand

landscape beneath the moon
on the arm of a man kneeling
in front of an abandoned church
darkness
at the mouths of alleys;
ring of water rising from an imagined
spring
theater of sand whose frontispieces crown
gables already in ruins by the time
of the Tudors;
empty terminal
where I collect these stones that I stroke
to perfection
and my shoulder
equidistant from train tracks
that will depart after
a landscape that gains or loses strength
kills us or revives us with its drift
whether it's on the surface of the paper
where I hide,
in the abandoned church
or in the Levant, everything sand.

ella volvía

ella volvía de su estéril landa,
bajaba a las piedras antes de que aquella intensidad
se convirtiera en sangre;
y todo aquel amor se convertía en sangre
bajaba por sus muslos (el camino que lleva al centro
es un camino difícil) es el reto del paso
de lo profundo a lo sagrado
de lo efímero a lo eterno,
porque esa intensidad se convertía en sangre
por su necesidad de ser librada en febrero
justo antes de la primavera
—de color apergaminado también sus muslos,
lo que llamaba a olvidar cualquier cosa
para ser un cuerpo también, un camino.
que uno atraviesa con las flores del vestido
convertidas en piedras
porque nada puede durar —ella lo sabía—
si no está dotado por un sacrificio.
la tierra está recientemente sembrada
(era la tierra de sus ancestros)
es el rito que se ejecuta cuando se construye un día
el deseo primordial de representarlo,
como si ese fuego y esas piedras
repitieran ademanes antiguos
y ella pagara con su flujo sobre la tierra estéril
para ser fecundada.

she would come back

she would come back from her sterile plain,
she would go down to the stones before that intensity
turned to blood;
all that love turned to blood
running down her thighs (the path toward the center
is a difficult path) it's the challenge of stepping
from the profound toward the sacred,
from the ephemeral toward the eternal,
because that intensity would turn to blood
in her need to be liberated in February
just before spring
—her thighs the color of parchment too;
she called on this to forget everything else,
to be a body too, a path.
which one walks with the flowers on the dress
changed to stone
because nothing can endure—she knew this—
if it's not provided through a sacrifice.
the land is recently sown
(it was the land of her ancestors)
it's the rite that one performs to build a day,
the primordial desire to represent it,
as if that fire and those stones
reproduced ancient gestures,
as if she paid with her flow onto a sterile land
to be made fertile.

a veces

a veces él y ella jugaban al escondite en torno
a los parvos de heno y los setos de ciruela podados
porque él entendía mucho de caballos y simientes
y olía a fruta desde el belfo a los cascos,
cuando sentado frente a ella con su abundante pelo amarillo
que estaba siempre tan revuelto como la melaza
y el agua de canela del tronco de aquel árbol de sus ojos
—de la supervivencia— eran los ojos que invadía la muerte
la sazón de la muerte con su espuma rojiza
(no hay palabra alguna para sacrificar la muerte
la muerte nunca está del lado de quien muere,
no señala su secreto en el acto de matar).
y ella entonces aportaba sus ojos que invadían la muerte
por encima de la sombra que entraba en el cieno.
yo tenía dieciséis años y lo veía venir
—lo abracé, como pude.
(debes olvidar toda argumentación, toda filosofía del desamparo)
me doblaba y mordía la punta de los dedos
tiznada de sagradas cenizas
bajo el calor de un sol meridiano
mi letra, su sílaba, simboliza el silencio después de la obsesión
—ella piensa en la divinidad.
no hacemos trampas.
el tiempo asesino le arrebata mi cuerpo y también
la abundancia del campo de la imaginación
donde todo fue amenazado
mientras la cosecha terminó de grabarse sobre el fango.

sometimes

sometimes they played hide-and-seek, he and she hiding in turn
among piles of hay and trimmed plum hedges
because he knew about horses and seeds
and smelled like fruit from his thick lips down to his hooves,
when he sat in front of her—abundant yellow hair
always as tangled as molasses,
eyes the liquid cinnamon of that treetrunk
—of survival—it was his eyes that death invaded,
the ripeness of death with its red froth
(there's no word to use for sacrificing death,
death is never on the side of the person who dies,
doesn't disclose its secret in the act of killing).
and then she would release those eyes that invaded death
in shadow flowing out over slime.
I was sixteen and I saw him coming
—I embraced him, as best I could.
(forget all argumentation, all philosophizing about abandonment)
I doubled up and bit into the tips of my fingers
sooty with sacred ash
under the heat of a dazzling sun
my word, its syllable, symbolizing the silence after obsession
—she thinks about divinity.
we're not playing games here.
the assassin, time, carries my body away and it
removes abundance from imagination's country
where everything was threatened
while the harvest left its final marks in the mud.

aguas raras (1981)

me siento en la rama más fuerte de la uva caleta.
me siento aquí (allá) donde está duro y cruje.
tomo el catalejo que la ola dejó abandonado.
—sólo algunos bañistas se oscurecen frente a mí.
el mar está sobrio y se mueve contra ellos.
espero otra inmersión —ellos juegan—
(hay verde oscuro suficiente para cubrirlos)
te he visto otra vez contra la resaca
silueta salobre, mano de arena, boca fría
y restos de quillas (ilusión) de lo que fueron
—otra muchacha con su vestido blanco doblando una pendiente—
pasión de contenerme en ella.
escapo a la playa y me siento en la rama más fuerte
de la uva caleta. está recia, torcida, petrificada,
sin dualidad ni sombra. deja que te contemple
tal vez se partirá.

strange waters (1981)

I sit down on the strongest branch of the sea grape.
I sit down here (there) where it's hard. it creaks.
I pick up a telescope abandoned by a wave.
—just some swimmers who darken before me.
the sea is temperate and it moves against them.
I wait for the next immersion—they play around—
(enough dark green to wash over them completely)
I've seen you against the undertow again
briny silhouette, sandy hand, cold mouth
and the wreckage of keels (illusion) of what they were
—another girl, her white dress curving down a slope—
passion to contain myself inside her.
I escape to the beach and I sit down on the strongest branch
of the sea grape. it's thick, twisted, petrified,
without duality or shadow. let me contemplate you.
maybe the branch will split.

algo será para mí

ver la mariposa amarilla y negra
sobrevolar la cabeza del perro
—no bisontes, renos, o caballos salvajes—.
ver la pelota roja junto al mar
equidistante entre la boca y su soledad.
ver mis uñas, me muerdo las uñas.
con mi mano acaricio la pelota, la barbilla del perro.
ojos que miran desde la orilla opuesta.
algas que sin ojos, ni bocas, se balancean con vida propia.
—algo será para mí—
el espacio que es urgente sobre la línea de flotación
atraviesa desde el agua un cuerpo indiferente
(el cuerpo mío, en mí, entre un período glacial y otro)
masas de hielo que alcanzan su máxima sabiduría
y al descender al nivel de los mares, se extienden
para hacer estos puentes terrestres.
(una llanura con bloques al sur y tundra).
ella emergió varias veces de las aguas
con su desfiladero peligroso.
me quedaré abierta, intacta, en la permanencia de las cosas.
la uña está partida y sangra.

something will be for me

see the yellow and black butterfly
fly over the dog's head
—no bison, reindeer, or wild horses.
see the red ball next to the ocean
equidistant from my mouth and its solitude.
see my nails, I bite my nails.
my hand rubs the ball, rubs the dog's muzzle.
eyes looking on from the other bank.
algae balancing without eyes or mouths, in life itself.
—something will be for me—
a space for urgency, just above the flotation line,
runs from the water across an indifferent body
(my body, inside me, between one glacial age and another)
icy masses that attain their maximum knowledge
then descend to sea level, spreading
to form these land bridges.
(a plain with blocks rising in the south, and tundra.)
she emerged several times from the waters,
from their dangerous passage.
I'll stay open, intact, in the permanence of things.
my nail is split. it bleeds.

bocas, destinos

como los anillos de esas bocas vacías
que han quedado flotando
pretendieron dibujar círculos en mis deseos;
como el sabor que es semi (dulce) semi (salado) semi (oscuro)
al temblor de mi saliva;
como la música que ella arrastraba desde el piano de fondo (mal)
y los residuos de otras bocas, otros destinos,
yo —empecinada en conquistar por una forma inmediata de algo—
la realidad que nunca me aceptó. me acerqué.
hasta ti llegaba mi acción dentro del humo
(sólo se quedan el humo y el silencio, y la vejez
como un paisaje)
la nadadora de aguas bajas que finalmente se lanzó
al océano para medir su profundidad.
no es definitivamente agria, ni oscura, ni dulce,
no es nada. ambigua se posa en el labio superior
de la composición. el sostén último a su fragilidad, ese océano
que enrosca su obsesión
de acortar la distancia entre el cuerpo y su lucidez
(el cuerpo que ya no pesa y se hunde sin remedio en el mismo lugar
encerrado para descender según el momento que atraviesa
con su masa inútil, su lentitud
un naufragio, donde el deseo se ahoga al final de la marisma).

mouths, destinies

like the rings of those empty mouths
that have kept on floating
they tried to draw circles on my desires;
like the flavor that is semi(sweet) semi(salty) semi(dark)
to the shaking of my saliva;
like the music she used to drag out of the piano in the back (badly)
and the residues of other mouths, other destinies,
I—stubborn about conquering immediate forms—
reality that never accepted me. I approached.
sallied out as far as you in the smoke
(only the smoke and the silence remain, and the old age
like a landscape),
the swimmer of shallow waters who finally threw herself
into the ocean to measure its depth.
it's not definitively bitter, or dark, or sweet,
it's nothing. ambiguous, she positions herself on the upper lip
of the composition. the last support for her fragility, the ocean
that coils up her obsession
with shortening the distance between the body and its clarity
(body that weighs nothing now and sinks hopelessly in place,
enclosed, to descend with the moment it passes
with its useless mass, its remains, its sluggishness,
a shipwreck, where desire drowns at the edge of a salt marsh).

el que se zambulle (1978)

la joven es Lili Brik compañera de Maiakovski
y hermana de Elsa T. cuando ella se zambulle
en la piscina de aguas azules y verdes
y soy ella entre otros relatos de amigos.
están, también mis padres en el pequeño bote
"El vencedor" que se vence sobre el mar encerrado
en una pecera. el que se zambulle, es también
otro, que nunca ha escrito un poema, ni tiene
otra jerarquía que su deseo inscrito
en el ceño fruncido de no ser alguno. el vencedor
(ése que se zambulle) y salta sobre el agua quieta
con su vaso de cerveza clarísima (Bavaria) congelada
entre los dedos es el tiempo. un personaje que siempre está
con nosotros, significando nosotros para nosotros,
cuando entramos en la turbulencia, o salimos a la paz
después de una guerra mental. tierra, agua, fuego, aire,
éter, discernimiento y egoencia, he aquí la
división de mi naturaleza, su instrumento.
el que se zambulle —manipulando la realidad,
la técnica de montaje, con su cámara oculta,
hace un esfuerzo en su inmersión para estar convencido
de que vuelve de allí, de algún paisaje irreal,
hasta encontrarse de nuevo el uno al otro
en ese pasadizo del alcohol
al final del cual, ella se queda quieta
(ella está al final de su vida)
quieta entre ellos y los otros;
mientras tu imagen se refracta
y se va acelerando el hundimiento de las islas
en las aguas azules y verdes…
la manipulación es tan antigua, que
el que se zambulle es el único inocente
que desconoce con su gozo, este experimento
interrumpido por la llegada de una ola…
(creo que cuando te suceda, si te sucede,
no lo sabrás).

the one who's diving (1978)

the young woman is Lily Brik, Mayakovsky's comrade
and Elsa T.'s sister, diving
into the pool with blue and green waters
and that's me between other stories about friends.
there too are my parents in the little boat,
"Victor," victorious over the ocean enclosed
in a fishbowl. the one who's diving is
someone else too, who has never written a poem, who has
no hierarchy other than the desire inscribed
in his brow, frowning about not being anyone. the victor
(that one who's diving) jumping over the quiet water
with his glass of Bavaria (light) beer ice-cold
in his fingers: time. a character who is always
with us, signifying us to ourselves
as we enter turbulence, or emerge into peace
after a mental war. earth, water, fire, air,
ether, discernment and ego-essence, here I have the
division of my nature, its instrument.
the one who's diving—manipulating reality
with his hidden camera, montage technique,
makes an effort by his immersion to be convinced
that he's coming back from there, from some unreal landscape,
to encounter her again
in that corridor of alcohol
where she stands, stilled, at the end
(at the end of her life),
still, between them and the others;
while your image refracts
and accelerates the collapse of the islands
into the blue and green waters...
the manipulation is so old
the one diving is the only innocent
who, in his joy, doesn't recognize this experiment
interrupted by the arrival of a wave...
(I think that when it happens to you, if it happens to you,
you won't know it.)

el pelo no se lo mojó. ningún rastro de agua salada en él. con los espejuelos muy oscuros y la toalla fresa sobre los hombros. entramos en el agua. al fondo, algas muy verdes, musgo y piedras que protegían de cualquier animal. una playa desierta, en la costa. viento y soledad. la arena cargada de caracoles muertos expulsados del mar contra mis pies. mi trusa malva y el pulover verde sobre el agua que apenas nos sobrepasaba las rodillas. él contemplándome; yo, arrastrando la sal de mi boca al fondo. deberíamos venir a pescar frecuentemente —le dije. hablamos poco. recuerdo, el temblor que provocó en mis piernas la carretera. mi mano en su hombro tan blanco y un roce de pelo arisco, como cuando uno limpia la mazorca de maíz hirviendo. pajuza rojiza. un olor a niño salado en la camisa (este hombre, el otro, que está conmigo aquí, me obligó a bajar las escaleras para proteger "su ilusión", no sabe cuál es mi venganza). lo vivo está en mi mente. allí, decoloro, o pinto cualquier imagen hasta la satisfacción. imagen salvada. hablamos algo sobre la libertad y aquellos lugares que uno escoge para colocar a diferentes personas, ya que no puede batirlas en un mismo coctel (odio a este hombre por su carencia total de metafísica). está terminando el día y a penas, algunas gotas levantan el calor del asfalto. pero en su boca hay una mordida interior que no se dio. sentados uno al lado del otro, bajo el chasis carcomido por la herrumbre, botas negras y zapatos verde manzana a cada lado. yo ensimismada en los tres caracoles que reposan sobre el muslo derecho —como tres anillos de s... no nos tocamos. no teníamos que hablar. él estaba impaciente por su pequeña estafa de hoy contra su proyecto de libertad (el pelo no podía llegar salado a casa) yo le pasaría la lengua pegajosa por la mazorca y no cabría duda. me habrían engañado una vez más. mi aprehensión desborda cualquier intimidad. es: "color conceptual" —diría alguien con petulancia. toco, los tonos vivos que tengo en la cabeza (un estado más adentro, al fondo, donde las algas se enredan contra mis piernas) mala palabra es ese animal que se enrosca y no se nombra nunca y hoy por tres veces se enroscó. ahora, lo escribo desde el tedio de sostener imágenes que podrían

his hair didn't get wet. no trace of salt water on him. with very dark glasses and the strawberry-pink towel across his shoulders. we got into the water. at the bottom, deep green algae, moss, and stones protecting us against any beast. a deserted oceanside beach. wind and solitude. the sand heavy with dead conchs expelled from the sea, hitting against my feet. my mauve swimsuit and the green shirt above the water that hardly covered our knees. he, contemplating me; I, dragging the salt out of the back of my mouth. we should come fishing a lot, I said. we spoke little. I remember the highway quivering through my thighs. my hand on his very white shoulder and a touch of shy hair, like when you clean an ear of boiled corn. reddish straw. smell of a salty child in the shirt (this man, the other one who's here with me, obligated me to go down the stairs in order to protect "his illusion." he doesn't know what my revenge is). what's alive is inside my head. there, I bleach out any image or paint over it to my satisfaction. image rescued. we talk about freedom and those places where you choose to locate different people now that you can't stir them into the same cocktail (I hate this man for his complete disregard of metaphysics). the day is ending and, faintly, some raindrops lift the heat out of the asphalt. but in his mouth there's an interior bite that didn't materialize. seated one next to the other, under the rust-chewed chassis, black boots and apple-green shoes on either side. me, deep in thought about the three conchs resting on my right leg—like three rings of the s...—we didn't touch each other. we didn't have to talk. he was impatient for today's little game with his freedom project (the hair couldn't go home still salty). I would move my clammy tongue over the ear of corn and there would be no doubt about it. they had deceived me again. my apprehension overflows any intimacy. it's "conceptual color"— someone would say, petulantly. I touch the vivid tones that I have in my head (a state further inside, in the depths, where the algae winds against my legs). the curse word belongs to the beast that coils up and never takes a name and it coiled up three times today. now, I write it, out of the tedium of sustaining images, sustaining

ser cualquier cosa colocadas en el espacio de mi felicidad. también hay truenos aquí, calor que ha levantado la lluvia y polvo. pero en mi mente, un cristal se abre y miro por su abertura un fragmento de mi lucidez. (mi papá también juntaba las piedras con formas de osos; también recogíamos aquellos cristales con formas de botellas vulgares que los bebedores echaban al mar devueltos como pulidas piedras verdes que se veían muy diferentes, cuando los echábamos en la pecera, cuando los encerrábamos allí). siempre había alguien esperándonos al regreso de estas travesías; alguien para borrar los pedazos de deseo; alguien para sostener y castigar (Foucault?) por qué ese miedo a la libertad del espacio diseñado por sus anillos nos trastorna hasta recurrir a la dualidad? como fondo mediatizado de la realidad —la piscina (la pecera)— el lugar donde hablábamos de lo que podíamos ser, o hacer, sin actuar, el lugar donde encerrábamos el presente sin darle continuidad. más adelante, el mar (salvaje, impreciso) donde el cuerpo recuperaría su libertad, o se perdería totalmente, lo que nunca aceptaríamos. en el presente continuo, el espacio de lo que somos —el último anillo de la s… en tierra— con su dolor y su vanidad, el mecanismo fácil de nuestra conciencia (la s… de dos cabezas). P me cuenta entonces, su relación con el muchacho, que ha debido venir —y yo, me envuelvo en su historia— como él con su sábana, en la toalla fresa. cuartos de mi cabeza, suburbios, pisos de ansiedad donde me escondo. pero estamos en un hotel, frente a un vaso de cerveza negra y ante nosotros, una mesa de calamina que imita un tejido de hierro calado y vulgar, el cuadro de esta piscina pálida y azul donde ni el agua intenta ser salobre ya; esa piscina que llevamos a todas partes. es lo normal. tú me cuentas la mecánica de esa relación con el muchacho —ningún estado sentimental— sólo ese relincho de las bestias que encuentro por las noches en mi cama. todo el calor a flote sobre las tres de la tarde sin relatividad en la engañosa piscina que es nuestro único poder, donde hacemos la fábula para dominar, ese temblor bajo las piernas sobre la bicicleta, mientras las gotas de lluvia levantan cuidadosamente otro vapor del asfalto.

anything, inside the space for my happiness. there are rolls of thunder here too, heat that raises rain, and dust. but inside my mind, a crystal opens and through its aperture I see a shard of my clarity. (my father used to gather stones in the shape of bears too; and we would collect glass crystals shaped like ordinary bottles, tossed by drinkers into the sea and returned as very different, polished green stones; we tossed them into the fishtank, we enclosed them there.) there was always someone waiting for us when we returned from these trips, someone to wipe out the shards of desire; someone to sustain and to punish. (Foucault?) why does this fear of spatial freedom, outlined by rings, unsettle us so that we resort to duality? as the mediated depth of reality— pool (fishtank)—place where we talked about what we could be, what we could do, without taking any action, the place where we enclosed the present without giving it continuation. farther along, the sea (wild, indefinite) where the body could recuperate its freedom, or where it could be lost absolutely, something we would never accept. in the continuous present, the space for what we are—the final ring of the s... on the earth—with its pain and its vanity, the easy mechanism of our consciousness (s... with two heads). P tells me then about his relationship with the younger guy, who should have come along—and I, I wrap myself in his story—like him in his sheet, in the strawberry-pink towel. rooms inside my head, marginal neighborhoods, floors of anxiety where I hide. but we're in a hotel, with a glass of dark beer, and in front of us is a zinc calamine table with a texture imitating common iron openwork, the picture of this pale blue pool where not even the water tries to be salty any more; that pool we take along with us everywhere. that's what is normal. you tell me about the mechanics of that relationship with the younger guy— no sentimental state—just the braying of beasts I find at night in bed. all the heat afloat over three in the afternoon, without relativity, in the deceitful pool that is our only power, where we make up a fable in order to attain dominance, that quivering under my thighs on the bicycle. as the raindrops carefully raise more vapor out of the asphalt.

el Kronan

el buque con todo el velamen desplegado
se inclinó a babor y zozobró
a merced del viento. el Kronan
con su mascarón de madera para atemorizar al enemigo
(los organismos que atacan a la madera
son menos abundantes que en las aguas más cálidas)
se hundió rápidamente (sobre el mar, cada ángulo
donde estuvo se marca ahora con una cruz blanca)
las esculturas siguen sujetas a la pared por clavos de hierro
que se oxidaron a poco del naufragio
y aún se encuentran en aquella posición
frías y recubiertas de cieno glacial.
(un siglo en miniatura se ha congelado frente a mí
el 1 de junio de 1976, al mediodía). somos nosotros sumergidos
abrazados a la viva piedra caliza
para sentir
el tiempo que pueden permanecer ausentes
las estatuas
en la baja salinidad del Báltico.

the Kronan

its sail completely unfurled, the ship
leaned to port side under the force of the wind
and capsized. the Kronan,
with a wooden figurehead for smiting fear into the enemy
(organisms attacking the wood here
are less abundant than in warmer waters),
sank quickly (above the sea, every angle it struck
is now marked with a white cross).
sculptures are still pegged to the walls with iron nails
that oxidized shortly after the shipwreck
and they remain in that position,
cold, covered in glacial sludge.
(a century in miniature has frozen in front of me
on the first of June, 1976, at noon.) we are submerged
clasped to the living limestone
in order to know
how long the statues
can remain absent
in the Baltic's low salinity.

la elegida

en esta tierra de polvo verde el Taj Mahal
es el guardián de la muerte
el sepulcro de la bien amada fallecida de parto
una mañana de invierno en el Agra.
la luminosidad del mármol atrae
a los peregrinos que acuden en la estación de las lluvias
cuando el resto de la tierra está seca
y sólo queda un reflejo
sobre las aguas (no sabemos hacia dónde movernos
si la superficie de la realidad es líquida,
o está sumergida; si la descifraremos de atrás hacia
adelante, para que todavía podamos significar
y en qué sentido significaremos) o esperar,
sobre esta tierra de polvo verde que es la vida
a que el clima haga el primer movimiento
en aquel lugar, donde fallecida de parto
una mañana de invierno en el Agra
hay una estatua, no la lucidez de un día;
hay una sombra, una falsificación,
que se parece a la verdad.

the chosen one

in this green-dust land, the Taj Mahal
is the guardian of death,
the sepulcher of the beloved dead in childbirth
one winter morning along the Agra.
the marble's luminosity attracts
pilgrims. they come in the rainy season
when the rest of the earth is dry
and only a reflection is left
on the waters (we don't know in which direction to move
if the surface of reality is liquid,
or if it's submerged; whether we should decipher it from back
to front in order to still make meaning;
how it is that we will make meaning) or do we wait,
in this land where green dust is life,
for the climate to make the first move
there, where dead in childbirth
one winter morning along the Agra
there's a statue, not the brilliance of daylight;
there's a shadow, a falsification,
that looks like the truth.

olympias

la flota griega sigue
la huella de Sinbad —el árabe legendario—
que con su tablilla de madera sujeta a una cuerda
mide las latitudes con relación a la caída.
al tamaño natural de las naves antiguas
2000 años después
con tres órdenes de remeros británicos
(los veleros resucitan en la copia que se fue a pique)
en el puerto de Apolonia
2000 años antes.

olympias

the Greek fleet chases
the trail of Sinbad—legendary Arab—
who measures latitude in relation to incline
using a wooden tablet hung from a string.
this is 2000 years after the fact,
at the actual size of the ancient vessels,
with three classes of British rowers
(sailboats return in the shape of the one that sank),
in the port of Apollonia
2000 years before.

a pique

el precio de un pequeño barco romano
en la ensenada de Lazaretto
—monedas de oro en bolsas de cuero
transformadas en concreciones marinas—
la concreción es lo que queda,
embarcación de la Edad de Bronce en Gelidonia
en el 1200 antes de Cristo;
un jarrón de porcelana Chi Ing pai
decorado con asas en forma de dragones,
procedente de algún templo hundido
donde está inscrito el nombre de Poncio Pilatos
—cal, tierra roja y piedra pómez volcánica—
rodean el nombre apenas descifrable
y si no recuerdo dónde
quedó la tierra aquella,
el farol junto a la ventana
el libro que nunca terminó de leer
en la mesa de al lado (Kavafis 1918)
la foto, un pequeño dolor, las mamparas azules
y contemporáneas
por donde ibas y venías
si no recuerdo dónde
un olvido mío nada significa.

sinking

the price of a small Roman boat
in the Lazaretto cove
—gold coins in leather pouches
transformed underwater into concretions—
the concretion is what remains,
embarkation of the Bronze Age in Gelidonya
in the year 1200 B. C.;
a porcelain Qingbai vase
decorated with handles in the likeness of dragons,
from some sunken temple
with an inscription: the name of Pontius Pilate
—lime, red earth and volcanic pumice—
these surround the barely decipherable name
and if I don't remember where
that faraway land was,
the lantern by the window,
the book he never finished reading
on the side table (Cavafy 1918),
the photo, a mild pain, the blue
contemporary screens
through which you were going and coming
if I don't remember where,
my forgetting signifies nothing.

le coin de table, hacia 1900

luna en cuarto creciente
se apagará
me apagaré
cuando esté llena.
(bebo agua igual que esta luna con su aro amarillo).
siete años me tocará sobrevivir
frente al gran espejo del salón
donde los dependientes cambiaron su turno de vivir
y esa pequeña mesa de madera oscura
con dos sillas oblicuas
reduciéndose
frente a mí.
(un lugar para dos, justo el espacio
suficiente para dos)
más lúcida, menos intensa, me sellaré
con el nuevo descenso de la luna en mi hombro.
queda una mancha
un té rojo deja una mancha
(la mancha cuya claridad lunar
socavaba mi especie cuando tú la besabas)
qué es lo que va a salvarse de nosotros,
los que vivimos pendientes de una mancha
cercana pero inalcanzable?
nadie la busca, nadie llega, nadie pretende.
víctima de su credulidad entre velas romanas
formando siluetas al borde de las cosas
fantasma de esta silla de enfrente
—alguien se fue—
y empezará septiembre otra vez
con luna rota
arabescos de metal
y vida de lenta derrota.
la concertista no ha dejado de tocar
siento el roce de su dedo metálico.
mientras la luna crece

le coin de table, circa 1900

quarter moon rising
will go dark
I will go dark
when it's full.
(I drink the same water as that moon hooped in yellow.)
seven years I will have to survive
facing the great mirror in the living room
where the dependents rotated through their lives
and that dark wood table
with two angled chairs
shrinking
in front of me.
(a place for two, just enough
room for two)
more lucid, less intense, I'll stamp
the new descent of the moon on my shoulder.
it leaves a stain
red tea creates a stain
(stain whose lunar clarity
undermined my kind as you were kissing it)
what is it that will save itself from us,
the ones whose lives hang on some
adjacent but unreachable stain?
no one looks for it, no one shows up, no one tries.
victim of her credulity among candles from Rome
forming silhouettes at the edges of things
ghost in this chair in front of me
—someone left—
and September will begin again
with a broken moon
metal arabesques
and the life of slow defeat.
the soloist hasn't stopped plucking at the strings
I sense the rubbing of her metallic finger.
while the moon grows

lentamente
se apagará
me apagaré.

slowly
it will go dark
I will go dark.

perdí una palabra

... perdí una palabra que me buscaba...
una palabra en la que de buen grado te perdí.

—Paul Celán

la palabra con la que uno camina se adelanta
a lo que uno camina. y uno ya es esa palabra
con una braza por delante a lo que viene detrás
que es el cuerpo... un volumen, un ademán,
aislado de su palabra que le abre paso sin que pierda el sentido
de ocupar el lugar de la palabra. una fortificación.
esta mañana ella me despertó
antes de mover los dedos, las pestañas, la brisa para sofocar
mi huevo y su luminosidad; para saciar un poco
el hambre de adelantarme a mí, retrocediendo,
sin encontrar un cuerpo que soporte su majestuosidad,
el derroche de sílabas repletas de labios
en el éter de pronunciar la redondez que habla del contorno
y provoca al fin esa palabra. (porque el gato tiene
dieciséis mutilaciones de palabras y su sonido
habla también de la palabra que perdí)
—la que me buscaba dentro de una marea de lenguajes—
y hubiera probado con lo que tengo en la garganta hasta reventar,
con lo que tengo en la mente como prueba de Dios,
hasta calcinar su voz junto al sonido
y fundirlo en algo que te convenza.
allí, donde estás,
cómo te mueves sin una cuerda, sin una fibra,
que te sujete?

I lost a word

I lost a word that was looking for me…
a word in which I willingly lost you.

—Paul Celan

the word with which one walks moves in advance
of the stride. and one already is that word,
a stroke ahead of what follows behind,
which is the body… a volume, a movement,
isolated from one's word, which opens the path without losing
    the sense
of occupying the word's place. a fortification.
this morning the word woke me up
before moving my fingers, my eyelashes, the breeze, to suffocate
my egg and its luminosity; to satiate some of
the hunger to surge ahead as I fall behind,
not finding a body to support its majesty—
the squandering of syllables, replete with lips
in ethereal pronunciation of the roundness that outlines
and finally provokes that word. (because the cat has
sixteen word-mutilations and their sound
speaks too about the word I lost)
—the one that sought me out in a wave of languages—
and with what I have in my throat,
with what I have in my mind as proof of God,
I would have tried until it burst,
until its voice charred along with the sound
and fused it into something that might convince you.
there, where you are,
how do you move without a string, without a thread,
to hold you?

patas de caballo

alguien asustó a las palomas en la Plaza de España
y levantaron vuelo contra mí.
la arena reseca bajo mis pies se agrieta
arriba ellas.
una ciudad está siempre en relación con nuestro amor
(estábamos allí para perder ciudades en sus grietas
y revivir encuentros que nunca ocurrirán.)
una camisa viaja por los letreros —es la postmodernidad—
el despilfarro de espejuelos que no ven más.
pero alguien asustó a las palomas en la Plaza de España
y en el centro de mi corazón ridículas sirenas
marcan la muerte con un sonido escarlata.
nadie me amó, ni me amará…
y levantaron su vuelo contra mí.

horse's hooves

someone scared the pigeons in the Plaza de España
and they rose up against me in flight.
parched sand under my feet cracks apart,
they're up above.
a city always exists in relation to our love
(we were there to lose cities inside their own fractures
and to relive encounters that will never happen).
a shirt speeds past through posters—it's postmodernity—
extravagant spectacles that project nothing greater.
but someone scared the pigeons in the Plaza de España
and at the center of my heart, ridiculous sirens
brand death with a shriek of scarlet.
no one loved me, or will love me…
and they rose up against me in flight.

anochece

anochece sobre las tejas de Madrid
pero en las manos traigo la humedad
de las aguas del Báltico.
todavía húmedas,
frías,
me han quemado con esos verdes que no maduran.
es la travesía desde los ojos de los cisnes
tras una fruta opaca. anochece
y estoy tan cerca de tu cuerpo en una casa extraña
contra los pies que en la madera quieren frotar
una textura adormecida sobre un paisaje irreal
(me han devuelto a la conciencia las palabras
que no están donde sueño o donde miro
busco un sueño donde están las sensaciones
porque ya no hay nada que mirar)
y busco algo que querer antes que la noche
irrite mis párpados que sobre las aguas del Báltico
han bebido toda su humedad. porque también anochece
sin prisa sobre las tejas de Madrid y yo miro
por la abertura oblicua de mi piel
la tuya.

night is falling

night is falling over the tiles of Madrid
but in my hands I bring the dampness
of Baltic waters.
still wet,
cold,
they burn me with pale greens that don't ripen
during white nights. it's the circuit from swans' eyes
following some opaque fruit. night is falling
and I'm so close to your body in a strange house
feet touching with their desire to rub a sleepy texture
into the wood, over an unreal landscape
(they've returned me to consciousness, the words
that are not in my dream or where I look,
I search for the dream where the sensations went
because there's nothing left to see here)
and I'm looking for something to want before the night
can irritate my eyelids that drank all the moisture
over the Baltic's pale waters. because night is also falling
unhurried over the tiles of Madrid and I look out
at your skin through the oblique opening
in mine.

en pleno mediodía

en pleno mediodía, las palomas
reacias al sol han bajado por sombra
y las parejas se abrazan tiradas en la hierba
húmeda y reseca del verano.
yo espero por ti que no eres nadie,
que no eres alguno,
bajo este mediodía cálido junto a la fuente
y comprendo la necesidad del querer
como los escalares
uno encima debajo del otro
en esta pecera sin fondo de la realidad.
(el loco de ayer ha vuelto —son recurrentes
los locos, los poetas—)
yo, con la misma ansiedad
también he vuelto a buscar mi sombra diurna
todavía puedo quedarme aquí
y no volver a otro sitio donde
una vez arriba, otra abajo,
intente derrumbarte contra la hierba
húmeda y reseca del verano.

at high noon

at high noon the pigeons
evading sun descend through shadows
and couples embrace, sprawled on summer's
damp, parched grass.
under this warm noon next to the fountain
I wait for you who are no one,
who are not anyone,
and I understand the necessity for loving
like scales
one on top under another
in this bottomless fishtank of reality.
(yesterday's lunatic is back—they're recurrent,
the crazies, the poets)
with that same anxiety, I'm
back in search of my diurnal shadow
I can stay here still
and not return to any other place where
one time on top, another on the bottom,
I might try to throw you down against summer's
damp, parched grass.

qué confusión

qué confusión me invade cuando despierto
y sé que estás cerca
qué confusión me invade cuando despierto
y no te puedo abrazar
hasta fundirme sudorosa al caos de las cosas.
el sonido de mi corazón (como patas de caballo)
golpea mi sangre acelerada por el vino.
qué confusión me invade
y no te puedo abrazar
—animal magnífico que inventé contra mi soledad
y que desprecio por ser tan vulnerable—
reseca está la arena donde ni un escombro
ha quedado,
sólo patas de caballo que levantan su dolor
con esfuerzo.

what confusion

confusion overwhelms me when I wake
and know that you're near
confusion overwhelms me when I wake
and I can't hold you tightly enough
to merge, sweaty, into the chaos of all things.
the sound of my heart, wine-sped,
pounds my blood (like a horse's hooves).
confusion assaults me
and I can't hold you
—magnificent animal I invented to challenge my solitude,
beast I scorn for being so vulnerable—
the sand is parched where not even rubble
remains,
just a horse's hooves, lifting the pain
with difficulty.

he venido

he venido a la Plaza de España sólo para ver
a la anciana de negro que se agacha
junto a la fuente
y acurrucando su cuerpo
contra el viento de abril en un gesto de actor que reduce
toda la compasión en su rigidez.
doblando
levemente las rodillas antes de actuar
antes de caer
ha traído ese alpiste blanco de los pájaros
que vuelven sucios
morbosamente a mí. he venido a la
Plaza de España sólo para recoger
lo que sobra de un gesto.

I've come

I've come to the Plaza de España just to see
the old woman in black who leans
by the fountain
huddled against the April wind
with the carriage of an actor, curbing
all compassion with her rigidity.
slightly bending
her knees before performing
before falling
she brings white seed for the filthy birds
that circle back,
diseased, to me. I've come to the
Plaza de España just to gather
something that overflows from a movement.

ella llama a eso... una mano. ella quiere hacer una
mano, en fin, algo, en alguna parte, que deje
huellas, de lo que ocurre, de lo que se dice,
realmente es lo mínimo, no...

—Samuel Beckett

the voice... calls that a hand, it wants to make
a hand, or if not a hand something somewhere that can leave
a trace, of what is made, of what is said,
you can't do with less, no...

—Samuel Beckett

mano de plata

el alcohol se ha derramado sobre la pequeña mesa y tu mano lo abraza por un momento, lo riega hasta llegar al borde y caer formando un mar de alcohol. un mar dentro del mar, donde sobresale tu anillo de plata grueso (un barco) flotando en medio de aquel océano de alcohol que ha puesto ebrio a los peces que en la plata quedaron atrapados. no puedo profundizar, ni horadar, la fotografía de tu mano; sólo puedo rozarla con la mirada y cubrirla como a una superficie quieta. la fuerza de evidencia de tu mano al expandir el líquido borra cualquier determinación. (ver topografiados los barcos, los peces, los crustáceos, con sus inmensas bocas, son cosas que conciernen a la realidad). el peligro de esa mano es que pone fin a cualquier límite que no autentifique la evidencia de tal ser. el aire de tu rostro está perdido por la restauración del orden que la mano ha querido disponer sobre la mesa. ya no te veo, desde que la mano era la verdad, la verdad para mí. todo alrededor se ha sumergido en una nueva forma de alucinación —por un lado no estar ahí, por el otro, haber estado siempre— con la fugacidad del dorso que mueve esa mano a la vez que refleja en la propela los fragmentos que absorbe de una evidencia rara. la música que desprende esa armónica y algunas teclas a la deriva en la boca de la mano, por un camino bordeando altamar, por una carretera de las películas de los cincuenta, arenosa, polvorienta y quebrada hacia la humedad. es precisamente en esta detención de toda realidad, donde comprendo por qué estoy sentada aquí, esperando ser movida por tu mano hacia el océano, como una copia de las que he sido en mí, o un reflejo bastardo de la pretensión de cualquier cosa que pretendí ser. tal vez estaba viva para probar, para certificar, un gesto así; el aire de un movimiento banal, el entreabrir los labios y mirar de frente el momento de la restauración en que ese pez vive contenido en la plata del dedo, abre la boca y salta apoderándose de mi deseo (de mi boca) de mi estancia pasiva y comprobatoria, de aburrirme al mirar de nuevo todo lo que vi para —aplazándolo— llegar hasta la evidencia de la red de una mano que además, puede tener las uñas sucias.

hand of silver

alcohol spills across the small table and your hand embraces it
for a moment, guides it toward the table's edge where it falls,
forming a sea of alcohol. a sea within a sea, centered on your
thick silver ring (a boat). it floats in the middle of an alcohol
ocean that intoxicates fish trapped inside its silver. I can't deepen
or pierce the photograph of your hand; I can only brush across
it with my gaze and create a smooth surface. the power of your
hand's presence, as the liquid expands, erases any decision. (see—
topographically—boats, fish, crustaceans, with their immense
mouths; these are things having to do with reality.) the danger of
that hand: it cancels out any boundary that doesn't corroborate
the evidence of its presence. the resemblance to your face
disappears with the restoration of order, worked by your hand on
the tabletop. I don't see you any more, not since the hand became
the truth, my truth. everything around it has been submerged
in a new kind of hallucination—from one angle, not being there
at all; from another angle, having always been there—with the
disappearing quality of the back side, the flip side that moves
the hand and simultaneously reflects fragments in the propeller,
fragments it absorbs from a strange kind of evidence. music
released by that harmonica and some strings, adrift in the mouth
formed by the hand. the music moves along a road bordering
the open sea, along a highway out of movies from the fifties,
sandy, dusty and breaking toward the moisture. precisely in that
suspension of all reality, I learn why I'm sitting here, waiting to
be advanced by your hand toward the ocean, like a copy of all
the women I've ever been inside myself, or like an illegitimate
reflection of the pretense of anything I ever tried to be. maybe I
lived in order to test out some gesture like that, to certify it; the
air of a banal movement, the half-opening of my lips and my turn
to face the moment of restoration, where a fish lives contained
inside the silver of a finger, the fish opens its mouth and jumps,
taking possession of my desire (of my mouth), of my passive and
observational waiting, of the way I get bored by looking again
at everything I saw in order to—postponing it—arrive at the

es el pedazo que ahoga esta mano en su mar de alcohol todo lo que yo amaba? es aquello que va a desaparecer para siempre? aquello abarrotado, donde no hay sitio ya para otros barcos, otros tesoros, otros navegantes? qué importa esta foto tomada del otro lado del simulacro de bar donde seamos representación pura, aplastamiento del tiempo, concreción (tampoco creo en la realidad de este momento, es quizás, un momento arcaico — como dirías). por estar muerto ya, por representarnos la fábula nuevamente de dos que se quieren besar y no se besan para encontrar otra cosa encerrada más adentro de la visión del besar. perdida en el fondo del alcohol miro —como el niño caído en el pozo cuya mano, la mano de una virgen azul levanta— la fuerza de una imagen transversal sacándome de allí —del fragmento de mar, del pozo reducido a poliedro de luz de donde vuelvo, sin más origen que esta desnudez probada de no saber decir lo que da a ver. este es el infinito campo de mi cuerpo (los vellos de los brazos que siempre escondí bajo la manga). el parecido conmigo es una conformidad con una identidad imaginaria. siento el horror del descubrimiento de los vellos de los brazos, de los vellos de las piernas, de las algas que basta limpiar para acceder a lo que hay detrás. basta limpiar la parte todavía ebria de la mesa, escrutar detrás del cristal, del papel, del sonido de la armónica sobre la carretera plana y polvorienta de un día, para alcanzar la cara inversa, el reverso de una mano, o tu sonrisa ante el parabrisas moviéndonos con exceso de velocidad (de densidad) hacia un tiempo que no tienen derecho a ser más que indiferente naturaleza y no a depositarnos constantemente en lo que ya no es. acción, con esa mano que abre el líquido en su mitad perfecta hacia la evaporación, mientras deja una grieta en mi labio que no ha podido morder fruta con alcohol (ciruela borracha) mientras menstruo y mi disfraz se desmorona con la nueva dirección que tu mano abierta señala sobre mí. sé que nuestro encuentro estaba acordado desde hacía muchos años y que ninguno de los dos contaba con el poder necesario para evadirlo, o para abreviar el lapsus según el cual miramos. porque sólo tú y yo —atravesando la hilera de diente-perros, los años, las diferentes líneas de árboles mudos e iguales a lo largo de la infinita distancia de una mano; las redes llenan de peces de plata petrificados allí, en el alcohol, rotundamente ebrios en tu

evidence of the hand acting as a net, which, moreover, may have dirty fingernails. this fragment drowned by the hand in its sea of alcohol: is it everything I loved? the thing that will disappear forever? the thing packed full, where there's no more room for other boats, other treasures, other navigators? what does this photo matter, snapped on the other side of the simulacrum of the bar where we could be pure representation, the flattening of time, concretion? (I don't believe in the reality of this moment either, maybe it's an archaic moment—as you would say.) by being dead already, by newly representing to us the fable about two people who want to kiss each other but don't, looking for something else enclosed deeper inside the vision of the kiss. lost in the alcohol's depths I look up—like the child fallen in a well, whose hand, the hand of a blue virgin, rises—at the power of a transversal image pulling me out of there—out of the fragment of the sea, out of the well reduced to a polyhedron of light from whence I return, lacking any origin other than this nudity, a nudity proven by not knowing how to say what it is that's showing. it's the infinite field of my body (hairs on my arms, which I always hid under a sleeve). its resemblance to me is conformity with an imaginary identity. I feel the horror of discovering hairs on my arms, hairs on my legs, algae that must be cleaned off to access whatever lies behind it. it's enough to wipe off the part of the table that's still intoxicated, to squint at what lies behind the glass, the paper, the sound of the harmonica above one day's flat and dusty highway, to get to the inverse face, the back side of a hand, or your smile at the windshield moving us with excessive speed (excessive density) toward a time in which they have no right to be anything more than indifferent nature, no right to drop us constantly inside something that doesn't exist anymore. action, with that hand opening the liquid into perfect halves moving toward evaporation, the hand also leaving a crack in my lip that can't bite through alcohol-soaked fruit (drunken cherry) while I menstruate and my mask crumbles with this new direction that your open hand signals over me. I know our encounter was agreed upon many years ago, and that neither one of us had the power to avoid it, or to condense the error through which we see. because it's only you and I—traveling across the row of sharp rocks sticking up out of the water, the years, the different lines of

dedo inseparable de la coartada de esa mano que ha tocado los cuerpos de barcos hundidos en la medianía del horizonte, sólo tú y yo, podemos mezclar en este momento la ficción de lo real y lo viviente entre las algas.

silent trees equal in length across the infinite distance inside one hand. nets fill with silver fish turned to stone there, in the alcohol, roundly inebriated in your finger, which can't be separated from the excuse of the hand that brushed against corpses of ships sunk at the halfway point of the horizon; just you and I, inside this moment, entwined in seaweed, we can blend the fiction of reality with the fiction of living.

como un álamo en una fila de álamos

ella fumaba unos cigarrillos Moore que eran suaves y oscuros. él tal vez pensó, que habría siempre otra caja para después. pero eran los únicos. a la distancia en que se encontraban no podía mirar de veras, si el brazo estaba allí después del garfio, o habría desaparecido por completo. (desde ayer me pregunto si alguien me ha querido alguna vez). la pérdida del brazo, ese olor peculiar de la goma que simulaba su mano, los guantes que la cubrían, me hacían pensar todo el tiempo en su boca. una huella trae el reclamo de un sendero y por él se encuentra todo lo demás. era extraño. durante días y noches soporté su conversación y su compañía. me hablaba de otros hombres a los que quería gustar. ella y él, sentados frente a la pequeña mesa de té, esperaban ser vistos, ser reconocidos (como un álamo en una fila de álamos) sé que la dejaba hablar sin escucharla. él sólo quería gustar para olvidar aquel error de nacimiento y apretaba la boca fuerte, fuerte contra el espejo y se miraba con una camisa de mezclilla azul profundo sobre el otro hombro —un hombro sin virtud. ahora, intentaba tomar algunos tragos de esa botella marrón —él pensaría también que habría otros tragos, otras botellas, otros brazos. no sospechó que era esta su prueba contra la decepción; su tránsito por ese pasillo del alcohol atravesando, una y muchas historias, para colocarse allí —de nuevo en situación errada, cubriéndose las costuras (de la cara, la mancha, el vientre) para colocarse allí frente a sus dos brazos —uno soñado y otro ausente, eterno; uno y otro puestos allí, frente a la nada convenida de cientos de excusas para llenar su desasosiego, su desolación, su desarraigo. esta vez él tenía sus dos brazos bien dirigidos a los lados del cuerpo y el cuerpo era una caja de resonancia; su costado —un músculo que se sospechaba desde afuera, un elegido de Praxiteles. ella sólo aspiraba a gustarle —como entonces, o desde siempre— desde que, por la punta del recuerdo abierto apareció su diente afilidísimo escondido tras la boca. (otra boca siguiendo siempre la huella de otras bocas, una más, Lena). eso es no tener propiedad, no pertenecer a un tiempo. ella insinuaba ser la que ofrecía un cigarrillo, un trago de alcohol, un poema, una imagen gastada

like a poplar in a line of poplars

she was smoking Moore cigarettes that were smooth and dark. maybe he thought there would always be another carton for later. but they were the only ones left. at that distance I couldn't really see if any of his arm was still left below the hook, or if it had completely disappeared. (since yesterday I've been wondering if anyone ever loved me.) the loss of his arm, the peculiar odor of the rubber simulating his hand, the gloves that covered it: these made me think constantly about his mouth. a trace left behind lures you toward a path and by following that, you find all the rest. it was strange. I put up with his conversation and company for days and nights. he talked about other men whom he wanted to please. seated at the tea table, he and she expected to be seen, to be recognized (like a poplar in a line of poplars). I know he let her go on talking without listening to her. he just wanted to give pleasure in order to forget that error of birth, and he closed his mouth tightly, tightly against the mirror and he looked at himself in the shirt with dark blue cloth over the other shoulder—a shoulder without virtue. now, he tried to take some swallows out of that brown bottle—he'd be thinking that there were other swallows, other bottles, other arms. he didn't suspect that this was his proof to stave off deception; his passage through a hallway of alcohol crossing one and many stories, to place himself there— again in an errant situation, covering up his scars (on his face, his stain, his abdomen) so he could place himself there, facing his two arms—one dreamed and another absent, eternal; facing the nothingness convened with thousands of excuses for filling his anxiety, his desolation, his uprootedness. this time he had both arms directed outward at the sides of his body, and that body was an echoing music box; his flank—its muscle suggested from the outside, a muscle chosen by Praxiteles. she aspired only to please him—like then, or like always—since, at the point of open recollection, her sharply pointed tooth appeared from its hiding place in the mouth. (another mouth always following the trace left by other mouths, one more, Lena.) that's what it means not to have properties, not to belong to any time. she hinted that

de su necesidad de ser advertida, identificada, consumida, en un plano contaminado y real por el deseo del otro (desde ayer me pregunto de madrugada si alguien me ha querido alguna vez) sabes por qué te acompaño desde entonces? por qué sostengo el garfio plateado contra el hierro, por qué me inclino y lo acaricio con tanta ternura? porque no ha podido abandonar aquella sensación de vértigo que por las noches entra en mi cuerpo y lo paraliza hacia el insomnio desgarrado que abre un paisaje común hacia su muerte árida, por donde regresan aquellas imágenes de lo que no fui, de lo que no tuve, de lo que estuvo tachado y sucio en alguna parte del texto para mí. es un aumento de potencia que termina en un aumento de impotencia. es el horror de vivir en un cuerpo (su vida) sólo por algo que es el abandono del amor, por el concepto absoluto del amor y correr tras una cosa que se acerca con apariencia de lo real y está mutilada y es otra falsificación. como si en esa dulzura de lo tardío —que es el recuerdo, mientras fumabas lentamente tu cigarrillo Moore con los dedos plásticos— como si en esa impostura estuvieran sucediendo continuamente, las postales, las poses, los juguetes, que sustituyeron siempre con su decorado de objetos perfectos a las personas de cerca y de verdad. yo disfrutaba el olor de la goma sudada que era su antebrazo; el borde redondeado del codo que moría sin hueso y sin ilusión; yo disfrutaba su angustia acariciando el guante doble amarillento que imitaba un color, una piel. lo que más me gustaba era trasladar aquella mano de metal con sus ajustes y correas al otro extremo del cuarto y depositarla allí, sobre la mesa, frente al espejo, que lo hacía múltiple. (un hombre que puede separarse de la inquietud de su mano derecha) verlo escribir sobre la pequeña Olivetti y rabiar contra las luces de la otra orilla donde comenzaba el mar que él no podía cruzar, eso lo distinguía. (ahora tengo que vérmelas con una estatua). cómo descongelar ese frío hielo del mármol? cómo se corrompe a una estatua? será el alcohol quien hará que las cosas se confundan cuando se acerque el final, la ebriedad y el desatino —dijo ella. algo tan morbosamente deseado cuando uno no quiere saber dónde ha quedado la otra parte del brazo de una estatua, que se complementa y reconstruye aquí y allá —y ella era una restauradora eficiente y tenía otra mano que se había albergamido en lo más hondo de su cuerpo para siempre; una mano

she was the woman offering a cigarette, a swallow of alcohol, a poem, an image expended in her need to be noticed, identified, consumed on a contaminated and real plane by someone else's desire (since dawn yesterday I've been wondering if anyone ever loved me). do you know why I've accompanied you since then? why I hold the plated hook up to the iron, why I bend over and caress it with such tenderness? because she hasn't gotten rid of the vertigo. it enters my body at night and paralyzes it with insomnia that rips a communal landscape open to its arid death, where those images of what I never was and never had can get back in, images of what was crossed out and dirtied for me in some part of the text. it's an increase in potency that ends with an increase in impotence. it's the horror of living in her body (her life) just for the sake of something equal to the abandonment of love, to the absolute conceptualization of love, running after a thing that approaches with the appearance of the real but is mutilated, another falsification. as if in the sweetness of something overdue—which is the memory of you slowly smoking your Moore cigarette with plastic fingers—as if in that imposture they were continually happening, the postcards, poses, games which always substituted their perfect decorative objects for real and present people. I took pleasure from the odor of sweaty rubber that was his forearm; the round edge of his elbow dying without bone or illusion; I took pleasure from his anguish, stroking the doubled, yellowish glove that imitated a tone, a skin. what gave me the most pleasure was to move that metal hand with its fittings and strips of leather to the other side of the room and drop it there, on the table, in front of a mirror that multiplied it. (a man who can separate himself from his right hand's worries.) to see him typing on the little Olivetti, raging against the lights from the opposite shore where the ocean that he could not cross began, the thing that distinguished him. (now I have to confront a statue.) how do you defrost that marble iciness? how do you corrupt a statue? it's alcohol that will confuse things with each other as the end gets closer, its intoxication and absurdity—she said. something so morbidly desired when one doesn't want to know where the other part of a statue's arm has ended up, or that it's complemented and reconstructed here, and there—she was efficient at restoration and had another hand sheltering

hermética y un brazo con boquetes abiertos a la razón plagiando una escritura caliente por dentro, hecha de innumerables manos que habían dejado sus huellas allí en fragmentos lúcidos. está ahí, muy cerca. cómo puedes vivir con eso?

permanently in the deepest part of her body; a hermetic hand and an arm with gaps open to reason, a hand plagiarizing fervent writings from the inside, a hand made up of innumerable hands that had left their traces behind in lucid fragments. the hand is there, very close by. how can you live with that?

memoria o estatua

... ha muerto un Dios cuyo culto consistía
en ser besado...

—Pessoa ("Antinoó")

la estatua de enfrente, a la distancia de mi mano, puede ser tocada suavemente. sus labios planos (único espacio de representación) realizan con mi gesto un vacío de palabras. no hay curiosidad, pero no puedo separar los dedos de esa boca de piedra caliza húmeda de alcohol, su sentido de la impasibilidad, de la inexpresividad es perfecto y me arrebata. la mano se detiene para que la estatua sea corrompida y baje su cabeza en una sacudida del sentido y la bese. (una sangría) él besa mis dedos ligeramente —oh, dedos diestros!— y por la noche, mucho después, desde el siglo de la resurrección (Cristo—Antinoó) en el silencio del Gran Escultor, ruedan los bloques de mármol, se precipitan violentamente, caen a mis pies, a centímetros de civilizaciones ya desaparecidas y yo, acaricio con mi mano izquierda, el lugar donde puso sus labios esa estatua, tan imposible ahora, porque todo en ella es ornamento de otro ornamento, fiesta de la resurrección. el lugar donde se espera un cierto estremecimiento de la persona, no está en los tejidos, sino detrás de la nuca, en cada vértebra que se desliza como un teclado. repito la caricia en mi mente, allí puedo pasar toda la noche acariciándome. pero, para ser exacta, lo que más impresiona del gesto de una estatua es un prolongado uso del deseo en la reiteración que se consume en pequeñas vibraciones o cláusulas al tacto, cuyos martinetes no rozan completamente atrás, no hay dolor, ya que no pretendan tocar o marcar un sonido. es sólo en ese sufrimiento de la fugacidad dentro del que uno espera la imagen de algún dios que parecía ser (su eco) que mis espasmos llegan con retraso, como el lento ensanchamiento y la contracción del big-bang después de milenios, casi al amanecer. él amanece conmigo, dentro de mí, lo he robado de otros tiempos y ruinas —como una ola cuya alquimia arrastró con la resaca, lo podrido, lo muerto, lo brutal y que, con su pequeña llegada al amanecer, empieza a traer cosas vivas dentro de una humedad

memory or statue

... The god is dead whose cult was to
be kissed...

—Pessoa ("Antinous")

the statue opposite, a hand's length away, can be touched gently. its flat lips (sole space of representation) empty out words with my gesture. there's no curiosity. but I can't take my fingers away from that mouth, made of limestone and wet with alcohol, its sense of impassivity, of inexpressivity, is perfect and captivates me. my hand pauses so the statue will be corrupted, lower its head in a tremor of sensation, kiss it. (a bloodletting) he kisses my fingers lightly—oh, skillful fingers!—and at night, much later, from the century of resurrection (Christ—Antinous) in the Great Sculptor's silence, the marble blocks roll, they plunge violently down, they fall to my feet, inches from vanished civilizations, and with my left hand I caress the place where that statue put its lips, so impossible now, because everything in it is an ornament of another ornament, a festival of the resurrection. the place where a little bodily tremor is anticipated. it's not in the body's tissues, but at the nape of the neck, in each vertebra that slips as if across a keyboard. I repeat the caress in my mind, there, I can spend all night caressing myself. but, to be exact, what is striking about a statue's gesture is a prolonged use of desire, the repetition that dissolves into small vibrations or clauses when touched, whose piano-hammers don't touch down in the back; there's no pain, because they don't try to play or score a sound. it's only in that painful fleetingness, within which one awaits the image of some god who seemed to be (his echo), that my spasms arrive late, like the slow expansion and the contraction of the Big Bang after millennia, almost at dawn. he rises with me, within me, I've stolen him from other times and ruins—like a wave whose alchemy swept the rotten, the dead, the brutal away in its undertow and which, with its humbled dawn arrival, brings living things in an excess of cold moisture. I still can't reach you, I can't get to you... one wants to steal the statue's security too,

fría en exceso. no puedo alcanzarte todavía, no puedo llegar hasta ti… uno quiere robarle también a la estatua su seguridad, su intemporalidad, rendir la flaccidez que me ha humanizado y agoniza el ser de carne que soy, sus grietas, donde estuvo impuesta la carga del sentido inútil de padecer frente a ella. uno quisiera participar por dentro de la restauración, abrirse para hacer de nuevo un corazón junto al busto de Adriano, tras otra larga agonía… "sobre el lecho profundo, por su desnudez total…" pero los dioses han impuesto una niebla entre él y yo. entre él y su pasado —cuyo culto consistía en ser besado— y mi propia figura corrompida y echada contra el lecho entre tantas formas perdidas de la experiencia, o de lo real. él me recuerda el efecto generoso del desastre; un rostro sin arrugas que invita a la suposición ficticia de pasar dentro de la historia violándola con esta escena inmóvil y cruel de la inocencia. entonces tiemblo. tiemblo en mi recorrido estático fuera del arte. él no dice nada. la imagen de nuestro amor atravesará los siglos. reconstruiré una estatua más allá de una vida opresa en vida, opresa en sentido; escribiré de nuevo el poema "Antinoó" de Fernando Pessoa; escribiré de nuevo las memorias de Adriano, te besaré en los museos y despertarás de la cultura muerta en el espacio prolongado de la representación que es tu boca, sus labios planos, como un mapa del exceso de ti.

its intemporality, to surrender the flabbiness that has humanized me, and the fleshly being that I am agonizes; its cracks mark the heavy, useless awareness of suffering in front of the statue. inwardly one would like to participate in the restoration, to open up and remake a heart next to the bust of Hadrian, after another long agony... "On the low couch, on whose denuded whole," but the gods have placed a fog between him and me. between him and his past—whose cult was to be kissed—and my own corrupt figure thrown onto the couch among so many lost shapes of experience, or of the real, he reminds me of the generous effect of disaster; unwrinkled face that invites the fictitious supposition of entering history, violating it with this motionless and cruel scene of innocence. then I tremble. I tremble in my frozen path outside of art. he says nothing. the image of our love will span the centuries. I'll reconstruct a statue beyond a life oppressed in life, oppressed in consciousness; I'll write Fernando Pessoa's poem "Antinous" all over again; I'll write Hadrian's memories all over again, I'll kiss you in museums and you'll wake from the dead culture in the prolonged space of representation that is your mouth, its flat lips, like a map of the excess of you.

un momento de negrura

para Minnie Marsh

siempre a las 10 de la mañana te encontraba cerca del parqueo. trucaba cientos de cosas antes de salir, cómo estaría mi rostro hoy, si había dormido bien, de qué hablaríamos, qué tiempo hace —no olvidar los espejuelos— cuánto dinero necesito, qué tal me va este color, cómo poner las venas dentro de las manos, absorber el refresco sin mancharme... a la distancia de mis ojos, otro rostro era siempre una censura, un bastión inexpugnable. a veces me contentaba tanto en las palabras que provenían del otro lado de la mesa, que sentía la formación de una nube mental (una burbuja) recreando las siluetas que formaban las imágenes de las imágenes, dentro de mis ojos. cuando ponía fin a este pequeño cine, me acordaba de ti y algunas veces de los otros. constantemente sentía el impulso obsesivo, abusivo —de abrazarte— de meter mi cabeza entre el desfiladero de la silla y la clavícula. allí descubría un pequeño lunar, una mancha de bronce, un lago para reposar y en el lago una flor, algo que estaría rozando después en el resto de las conversaciones estúpidas sin que los otros vieran, que mis ojos miraban hacia abajo, que acariciaban y sonreían al país de aquella mancha. claro, que saldría rápidamente del abrazo. qué haría yo con un abrazo así? enrojecer, mitificarlo, recordar... por las noches, la tensión de la energía recibida que me llevé (sin dar) no me dejaba dormir. como coágulos —dirías tú— se concentraban en mi interior dando punzadas bajitas, cabriolas en mis piernas y zumbidos de abejones en mis oídos. creo que he podido mirarte bien. creo que puedo recordar a la perfección, tu cuerpo y lo que está retenido en tu rostro. también creo, que hemos llegado al clímax, al broche de oro, de una red de metáforas y de hechos que concluyen en este deseo final. no sé por qué: te quiero abrazar... pero esa frase solemne, que reivindica toda mi vida es la frase con la que rezo a Dios siempre hacia el borde de la silla, con la pierna derecha cruzada sobre la izquierda (contra el tumor, el miedo, el ovario, la cruz) empujando a Dios, pidiéndole que me salve. pero

a moment of blackness

for Minnie Marsh

at 10 in the morning I would always find you near the parking lot. I would go over hundreds of things before leaving, how would my face be today, had I slept well, what would we talk about, what's the weather like—mustn't forget my glasses—how much money do I need, how well does this color suit me, how to make the veins in my hands disappear, how to drink my soda without getting it all over myself... from this distance, another face was always a censure, an unassailable fortress. at times I contented myself so much with words that originated from the other side of the table that I felt the formation of a mental cloud (a bubble), recreating silhouettes that images of images formed in my eyes. when I put an end to this miniature film, I remembered you and sometimes the others. I constantly felt the obsessive, abusive impulse—to hold you—to fit my head into the ravine between the chair and your collarbone. there I discovered a small mole, a bronze stain, a lake for relaxation and in the lake a flower, something that I would later stroke during the rest of the stupid conversations without the others noticing that my eyes looked downward, that they smiled at the country where that stain was and caressed it. of course, I would exit the embrace rapidly. what would I do with an embrace like that? blush, mythologize it, remember... at night, the tension of the received energy I took for myself (without giving) kept me from sleeping. like clots— you would say—they concentrated themselves inside me, pricking me gently, skipping in my legs, and buzzing in my ears. I think I've been able to take a good look at you. I think I can remember, perfectly, your body and what your face retains. I also believe we've arrived at the climax, at the gold brooch, of a web of metaphors and facts concluding in this final desire. I don't know why: I want to hold you... but that solemn sentence, which vindicates my whole life, is the sentence with which I pray to God, always on the very edge of my chair, with my right leg

cuál es mi Dios, cuál es el Dios de Minnie Marsh? llegábamos siempre en la bicicleta hasta el parqueo, donde la perra ámbar daba de mamar a sus perritos y entrábamos al hotel, decíamos "para dejar una crónica de su reconstrucción". el tragaluz, que tenía flores de colores me afectaba, no sabía qué lado de las sombras era más favorable a mi imaginación, a mi perfil. casi rígida, ella, Minnie Marsh, había llegado de Inglaterra, de la antigua Inglaterra de Virginia, de mi libro de relatos completos, con sus ojos gastados de ver tantos derrumbes, de abrir tanto el bolso y sacar la flor ajada y seca del vestido de terciopelo (de tu mancha)... yo también tengo mi flor! una flor es una recompensa que uno ha guardado contra los abusos de la superficie, contra los malos pensamientos de un "cualquier algo"; contra los límites de las rocas donde la visión podía deshacerse junto a las demarcaciones de la percepción, del signo y de la imagen. una flor existía para mí, me demostraba que esto ha sido, flota sobre la orilla del régimen atroz del amor. hace unos segundos que ella entró en tu cuerpo, en tu voz, en tu mente, en tu espíritu, tal como ella era en sí misma. está allí y es todas aquellas que en tu corteza de hombre puedas sostener desde una idea, o desde tu pene altísimo. quién dijo que era única? los rostros llevan las máscaras de lo que fueron, el guión y la censura de todos los rostros que participan siempre hasta el final; como los objetos llevan el alma, la pasión y hasta el descuido (el desenlace) en las protuberancias, de los símbolos que formaron, de los elementos que hallaron para su fusión. estamos aquí, otra vez en el proceso de la combustión, no sé por qué entraste en esta historia; no se por qué bajaste del tren que atravesaba los Alpes Suizos para estar aquí, junto a la iglesia gótica con sus rosetones que retienen hacia adentro amor y miedo, bajo los picos nevados del aire acondicionado del lobby de un hotel. no sé por qué, tu piel se hace más pálida cuando la miras, a medida que se aproxima, acerca y aproximan las doce campanadas y yo toco los cuadros de caballeros antiguos, yendo así de foto en foto, de jinete en jinete sin apocalipsis, de relieve en relieve para reconstruir la mano en su densidad, la mano en su profundidad, tal vez entre la tumba de algún faraón, o entre los restos de un naufragio que se ha consumido sin una imagen justa entre las algas. ahora, quizás, estás aquí, probablemente también reconstruyendo tus mentiras con las que formas tu pose votiva

crossed over my left (against the tumor, the fear, the ovary, the cross), pushing God, asking him to save me. but who's my God, who's the God of Minnie Marsh? we always used to bike to the parking lot, where the amber bitch nursed her puppies and we entered the hotel, as we said, "to leave a chronicle of its reconstruction." the skylight, which had red-colored flowers, affected me, I didn't know which side of the shadows was more favorable to my imagination, to my profile. almost rigid, she, Minnie Marsh, had arrived from England, from Virginia's old England, from my book of complete tales, her eyes exhausted from seeing so many collapsed buildings. from opening her purse so often and taking the crumpled, dry flower out of the velvet dress (out of your stain)... I too have my flower! a flower is a reward that one has guarded against the abuses of the surface, against the bad thoughts of "whatever"; against the limits of rocks where vision could undo itself next to perception's demarcations, of the sign and of the image. a flower existed for me, it demonstrated to me that this has been, it floats above the shore of love's atrocious regime. a few seconds ago she entered your body, your voice, your mind, your spirit, such as she was in herself. she is there and she is all of them whom, in your manly exterior shell, you can support from an idea, or with your most erect penis. who said she was unique? the faces wear the masks of what they were, screenplay and censure of all the faces that always participate until the end; like the objects wear the soul, the passion and even the neglect (the outcome) in lumps of symbols that they formed, elements they found for their fusion. we are here, again in the process of combustion, I don't know why you entered this story; I don't know why you got off the train crossing the Swiss Alps to be here, next to the gothic church with its rose windows holding love and fear inside, beneath snowy peaks of air conditioning in a hotel lobby. I don't know why; your skin pales when you look at it, as you get closer, draw near, and the twelve peals of the bell get closer and I touch the portraits of ancient gentlemen, going like this from photo to photo, from horseman to horseman without apocalypse, from relief to relief to reconstruct the hand in its density, the hand in its depth, maybe, in some pharaoh's tomb, or among the remains of a shipwreck consumed without a just image in the seaweed.

(que es casi el compromiso de una vida) mientras yo te dibujo con la mano izquierda (tántrica) y toco tu ombligo debajo del pulover sudado y deshago todos los ovillos hechos por anteriores caricias, desde mi rincón de ser otra historia de Minnie Marsh (no era ella y sin embargo tampoco era otra persona) otra culpa de Minnie Marsh, que por descuido de su reloj infantil dejó caer a su hermano, a su queridísimo y único hermano de esta altura — porque yo estaba mirando una franja de tierra en la frase mientras él caía; o tal vez su padre se enamoró de "brillito de oro", como él la llamaba y no lo dejó quererla con sus celos de niña insuficiente, cuando lo ahogué en el río que arrastraba toda un vida (no la mía) sino de aquel a quien yo amaba en la oración. tal vez la obsesión de retener a todos estos hombres es no haberme entregado a ninguno —como Minnie Marsh sin rastro de sexo... qué se yo. cuando mueves la boca sé que estoy a esa inmensa distancia, de aquel fragmento de espacio y tiempo que es una vida. tendría que reconstruir escombro tras escombro, esas ruinas y volver a los parques, a los quicios, a las terminales con sus bancos húmedos donde me senté con una flor de ocho pétalos que es siempre virtualmente loca porque no mira nada presente y hace al mismo tiempo efecto de verdad, cuando retiene aquella mancha de bronce insignificante que es al fin su destino. pero es otra vez ese rostro de Minnie Marsh entrando en la historia, con sus botas abotonadas de nieve y la mancha de un gran acontecimiento que ocurrirá mientras miro tu nuca y ella no cesa de imitarme dentro de tus ojos —otra vez champaigne— es ese acontecimiento, que por no ocurrir nos distorsiona los significados y se disuelve en un mal erótico y en una palidez que nos puede arrastrar a mí, a ella, tras el misterio de la simple concomitancia. tal vez hacia una ruina que no es de bronce, o de oro y quizás sea totalmente plástica y vulgar. en los momentos en que decaigo de este sentir pongo la proyección de la literatura y eso también cumple el sinuoso trayecto de mi línea. el temblor de una mano que se levanta para asegurar alguna cosa y se vuelve a posar (de esta forma no se me ven las venas) mi sangre se coagula sobre aquellas figuras de yeso, ha pasado por millones de años para aprender su inflexibilidad, ese juego de la luz a través del rosetón de lata por donde filtra el sol esta mañana lo que quiere. has encontrado a esta clase de mujer despiadada, que quiere ser cualquier mujer y

now, perhaps, you are here, probably also reconstructing your lies out of the ones that form your votive pose (which is almost the commitment of a life) while I draw you with my left hand (tantric) and touch your bellybutton beneath your sweaty polo shirt and undo all the tangled lint made by previous caresses, from my angle as another Minnie Marsh story (not her and yet not anybody else), something else to blame on Minnie Marsh, that by a slip of a child's clock she let her brother fall, her dearest and only brother, from this height—because I was staring at a strip of the sentence while he fell; or maybe her father fell in love with "little ray of gold," as he called her, and she didn't let him love her with the jealousy of an inadequate girl, when I drowned him in the river that dragged away a whole life (not mine) but that of the other person whom I loved in prayer. maybe from obsessively retaining all those men comes not giving myself to any one—like Minnie Marsh without a trace of sex. what do I know. when you move your mouth I know I'm at an immense distance from that fragment of space and time which is a life. I would have to reconstruct debris piled on debris, those ruins, and I would have to return to the parks, to the doorjambs, to the terminals with their damp benches where I sat with an eight-petalled flower that's always almost crazed because it doesn't look at anything present and creates at the same time an effect of truth, when it retains that insignificant bronze stain that is finally its destiny. but again it's that face of Minnie Marsh entering the story, her boots buttoned up in the snow, with the stain of a great event that will happen, while I look at the nape of your neck and she still imitates me in your eyes—again champagne—it's that occurrence, which by not occurring distorts the meanings for us and dissolves into an erotic evil and a pallor that can drag us, me, her, behind the mystery of a simple concomitance. maybe toward a ruin that isn't bronze or gold and perhaps is thoroughly plastic, vulgar. while this feeling wanes in me, I project literature as a movie and that too completes my line's sinuous trajectory. the twitching of a hand that rises up to secure some thing and returns to rest (in this manner my veins can't be seen), my blood coagulates on those plaster figures, it has passed through millions of years to learn its inflexibility, that play of light through the tin rose window where the sun filters

todas las mujeres. no me dejes echarte en el cesto de las culpas, hay demasiada cultura en mi obsesión de velar por la belleza de su fealdad. Minnie, Minnie Marsh, con su rostro cubierto de polvos Mirurgia, su sombrerito con el ave del paraíso colgada pero sin volar desde la ventana. ah, ahí está también esa ventana-mirador que no tiene lugar y que no cesa de invitarme. yo siempre estaba en el alféizar, justo en el espacio de no ser paisaje, de no provocarme una inversión en el contorno de unos ojos... "los ojos de los demás son nuestras cárceles, sus pensamientos nuestras jaulas..." cómo hacer un lugar para no diluirme completamente en ti? me aferro al alféizar insinuando que nadie me permitió entrar o salir y como esa mariposa —más bien un ave acuática del paraíso del sombrero de Minnie— no bajar, no mojarme. seguir así, columpiándome (ave por arriba, ave por abajo) en esta altura fingida por el miedo. mientras tanto, pensaba cómo sentir que quería abrazarte y no salir nunca de esta frase, buscando el sostén de esa columna vertical y gótica de esos huesos más fuertes de las letras; mientras mi boca se negaba a pronunciar algo, más fruncida, más apretada a la hilera de dientes de abajo, que se ven cada vez más con los años (uno empieza a morder desde abajo) y algo se ennegrecía allí, para hacer la larga noche de mi boca; me petrificaba como un oscuro yacimiento de saliva en mi postura señorial de Minnie Marsh, acercándose a un hombre alto y pálido que al abrazarla le acercaba un bastón para que no cayera aquel esqueleto de joven que quería entregarse todavía y para cuyo momento de negrura la piel ya no respondía y cerraba la boca, apretaba los labios, que antes fueron rosados y gruesos. (jamás podré escribir una novela. para escribir una novela necesitaría abrir esa ventana para que entraran bandadas de pájaros oscuros; tragar y engullirme las tóxicas opciones que tuve y no acepté. tendría que descruzar la pierna derecha de su cruz y decidir de qué lado del alféizar que hemos hecho, estar. seguir más allá del pliegue de la boca fruncida de su vestido gris de terciopelo y engullirme el pasado de otras bocas —como la tuya— dentro de tal oscuridad. tal vez, ya no sea posible devorar tanto tiempo acumulado.) cuál es el Dios de Minnie Marsh? el Dios de los callejones? el Dios de la vejez? el Dios de las tres de la tarde? yo también veo tejados, veo tu boca, que no me atrevo a tocar. pero, ay, no tengo ningún Dios en qué pensar, o cómo, de qué forma,

whatever it wants this morning. you've found this kind of ruthless woman, who wants to be any woman and all women. don't let me throw you into the basket with the blame, there's too much culture in my obsession of keeping watch for the beauty of her ugliness. Minnie, Minnie Marsh, her face covered with Mirurgia powder, her little hat with the bird of paradise hanging in but not flying from the window. ah, there is also that window—a bay window which has no place and still invites me. I was always on the windowsill, right in the space of not-landscape, of not-provoking in me an inversion contoured by eyes... "the eyes of others our prisons, their thoughts our cages..." how to create a place so I won't dilute myself completely in you? I cling to the sill, insinuating that nobody allowed me to enter or depart, and like that butterfly—rather, like an aquatic bird of paradise from Minnie's hat—to not-descend, to not-get-wet. to continue like this, swinging (bird above, bird below) at this height feigned by fear. meanwhile, I wondered how to feel that I wanted to hold you and never leave this sentence, seeking support for a vertical and gothic column of those stronger bones of words; while my mouth refused to pronounce anything, more wrinkled, more firmly pressed against the fine line of lower teeth, which are even more visible with the years (one begins to bite from below) and something was turning black there, to make my mouth's long night; it froze me like a dark deposit of saliva into my stately Minnie Marsh stance, approaching a tall, pale man, who upon embracing her gave her a cane so her youthful skeleton, which still wanted to give itself, wouldn't collapse, and to whose moment of blackness her skin no longer responded, and her mouth closed, her lips pursed, which before were pink and thick. (I'll never be able to write a novel. to write a novel I would need to open that window so that flocks of dark birds could enter; I would need to swallow and gulp the toxic options that I had and didn't accept. I would have to uncross my right leg from its cross and decide on which side of the sill that we've made I should be. continue beyond the fold, the frowning mouth of her gray velvet dress, and swallow the past whole out of other mouths—like yours—in such darkness. maybe it's no longer possible to devour so much accumulated time.) who's the God of Minnie Marsh? the God of the back streets? the God of old age? the God of three in

con qué color imaginar que pienso en él. cuál será la frase final que fingiré decirle un segundo antes de morir… te quiero abrazar.

y fue el aliento del refresco el que la petrificó y la convirtió otra vez en estatua de sal por haber pedido demasiado.

the afternoon? I too see tiled roofs, I see your mouth, which I don't dare touch. but, oh, I don't have a single God to think about, or a way, in what form, with what color to imagine that I think about him. what will be the final sentence that I'll pretend to say to him one second before dying… I want to hold you. and it was the whiff of soda that froze her and changed her back into a pillar of salt for having asked too much.

hay un lugar

un antílope negro empuña la razón
en el regazo de ella
donde está el hombre de tres ojos que la sigue
el que extiende los brazos en ademán de otorgar.
de color ahumado, el mándala con el triángulo invertido
que reluce de fulgores, el rayo
es el luto del corazón que está rojo o está dorado,
cuando lo suavizan con néctar.
hay una media luna en su cabeza
es de color oro
debajo de él es como la tranquila llama de una lámpara
ese árbol, el lugar del culto mental.
no he hecho otra cosa que describir mi corazón
—como en los libros sagrados, un diagrama—
desde niña lo sentía crecer y palpitar
(su mirada es jubilosa y denota ímpetu y deseo).
a veces permanecía sentada con la mano izquierda
inclinada hacia él. tú lo tocas
y se humedece el loto de ocho pétalos
con la cabeza hacia arriba. te está mirando.
espera tal vez, algo de ti.
en el regazo de ella
hay un hombre sentado que extiende los brazos
en ademán de otorgar
es su corazón
—la flor, en su abandonado altar de pétalos—
que aún no se ha preparado bien para morir.

there's a place

a black antelope wields the reason
in her lap
where the man with three eyes follows her,
the one who extends his arms in a gesture of devotion.
the shade of smoke, the mandala with an inverted triangle
that glitters and sparks, this flash
is the mourning worn by a heart, it's red or golden,
when they soften it with nectar.
on his head is a half-moon
its color is gold
under him, tranquil as a lantern flame
that tree, location for the mind's worship.
I've done nothing more than describe my heart
—diagrammed it, as in sacred texts—
since childhood I've felt it expanding, palpitating
(its gaze is jubilant and denotes energy and desire).
sometimes I stayed seated with my left hand
tilted toward it. you touch it
and the eight-petalled lotus dampens,
its head rising upwards. it's looking at you.
maybe it hopes for something from you.
in her lap
there's a seated man who extends his arms
in a gesture of devotion.
it's her heart
—the flower on its abandoned altar of petals—
that still hasn't prepared for death.

un vidrio, en la ventana

él hacía ventanas con fragmentos de vidrio
recogidos del mar. (el color ámbar
detrás del vidrio desdibuja mi rostro,
su falsedad) sostener mi figura
rehacerla y romper
la miniatura de ser con la que conviví.

no regresar a ella para huir lentamente
en el límite de cada fragmento dispuesto
entre tus manos
como otro vidrio fundido en la ventana.

a pane of glass, in the window

he melded glass shards collected from the sea
into windowpanes. (the color of amber
behind the glass blurs my face,
its falsity.) hold my figure
remake it, smash
the miniature self, the one who coexisted with me.
—not returning to her, escaping slowly
into the border of each fragment arranged
between your hands
like another shard melded into the windowpane.

en la estación Sud Este de Beckett

será hacia el sur
a través de largos raíles
que nos encontraremos.
la gente que nos acompaña
no saben, ni quieren saber
del precio de esos rosetones
que filtran la luz
intermitentemente
bajan la cabeza y caminan
alrededor
fingiendo que no la ven.
nosotros sobrevivimos
con palabras sujetas a otra pérdida
a lo largo de esos raíles
llevando una cabeza contemporánea
como paradigma del género humano.
ser otra cosa, un estilo, alguna filiación
sin oídos, sin voz y sin ser
cambiando de clase
(yo, en mi vagón que se ha descuidado
del tiempo y del lugar pienso
con el aliento en ti; pienso
con la sangre en ti) y acaricio tu
mano en el oscuro día de los andenes
parapetados en la estación Sud Este de Beckett
con el tiempo justo en medio de un gran tiempo
que se va borrando junto a la ventanilla
por donde asoma el tiempo de lo real.
porque las ciudades que hemos visto
no son eternas al final de noviembre
(y un acechador tiene un solo propósito
ante la conciencia de su muerte
mirar en el presente de las cosas con
intensidad) y pasar desapercibido
hacia el lugar donde

in Beckett's South-Eastern Railway Terminus

it will be in the south
having followed long tracks
where we'll meet.
the people who accompany us
don't know, don't want to know
the price of those rose windows
that filter light
intermittently
they drop their heads and walk
around
pretending they don't see the light.
we survive
with words subject to another loss
at the end of those tracks
transporting a contemporary head
as a paradigm for humankind.
to be another thing, a style, some filiation
without hearing, without voice, without self
changing class
(in my train car that has neglected
time and place I think through
the breath in you; I think through
the blood in you) and I stroke your
hand in the gloomy daylight of the platforms
sheltering in Beckett's South-Eastern Railway Terminus
at a time halfway to a greater time
blurring near the window
that frames the time of the real.
because the cities we've seen
are not eternal at November's close
(and an observer has a single purpose
in the awareness of his own death:
to view the present tense of things with
intensity) and to move unperceived
toward the place where

un día nos encontraremos
allí, donde la vida persiste
donde toda vida ha desaparecido
a través de largos raíles.

one day we'll meet,
there, where life persists
where all life has disappeared
along the tracks.

la foto del invernadero

fue la que siempre quisimos y faltó.
el invernadero estaba junto al parque
con sus cristales húmedos bajo el sol que entraba
en la tarde, o en la mañana, a colorear sus plantas.
yo me paseaba contigo de la mano —eras
de estatura un poco más bajo que yo—
y así alcanzaba a ver, desde esa altura,
los tallos quebrados por mi madre
que componía y podaba las macetas de buganvillas.
nunca entramos, éramos demasiado pequeños
para invadir la zona de confianza de esos seres extraños
que permanecían dentro. estábamos afuera.
saltando con nuestra energía sin razón
excluidos de la paciencia de las manos de mi madre
pero es allí donde quisiera vivir…
en el lugar inexacto de una foto que falta
para que no imite otra vez, o intente imitar el ser que soy.
el paisaje prohibido donde pondríamos el amor
con exclusividad.
el paisaje del deseo, que no se superponía o se reproducía
    a cada instante
y que permaneció oculto para nosotros
—la algarabía de ser niños no nos dejaba ver
"todos andábamos a la caza de una flora insectívora".
éramos suspicaces. ahora, acomodo en mi mente
la mente del invernadero. su llama tibia
en el centro de las imágenes haciéndonos creer que algo temblaba
o que podría no ser alcanzable.
esa incertidumbre del temblor donde cruje la madera
y la realidad se distorsiona y parte en dos lenguajes.
fue la que siempre quisimos y faltó.

9 de marzo de 1995

the winter garden photograph

it was the one we always wanted, and it wasn't there.
the winter garden was next to the park.
sun descended through condensation on its panes
in the evening, or in the morning, bringing color to the plants.
I walked hand in hand with you—you were
a little shorter than me—
so I was tall enough to see
the stems broken by my mother
who arranged and pruned the bougainvillea.
we never went in. we were too small
to trespass on the trust of those strange presences
inside. we stayed out.
jumping with our senseless energy,
excluded from the patience of my mother's hands.
that's where I'd like to live…
in the inexact place of a missing photo
missing so it can't replace or essay the person that I am.
the forbidden landscape where we would place love
exclusively.
the landscape of desire, not superimposed, not reproduced
    moment by moment,
one that remained hidden from us
—the uproar of childhood kept us from seeing that
"the plant we were all hunting was carnivorous."
we had our suspicions. now, in my mind, I make space for
the mind of the winter garden. its warm flame
at the center of the images convincing us that something inside
    was quivering
or might have been unattainable.
the uncertain quivering where the wood creaks,
reality contorts and splits into two languages.
it was the one we always wanted, and it wasn't there.

March 9, 1995

una casa encantada en la esquina de San Rafael

... iban de habitación en habitación cogidos de la
mano, levantando aquí, abriendo allá, cerciorándose...
una pareja de fantasmas...

—Virginia Woolf

una casa encantada no descubre fácilmente sus anteriores
encuentros; no delata la intimidad de la pareja que la habita. la
ropa colgando de las puertas, la cama a medio hacer y el reloj que
sigue su ritmo imperturbable. tú, estás allí cuando llego y nos
sentamos en dos sillas de madera gruesa. (no sé todavía cómo
entrará la luz en la mañana.) mis medias negras se alisan entre
la mano y tu boca sobre el pie que tú prefieres. hace frío. ella nos
observa. él también se cruza con mi imagen desde el espejo, para
recordarnos que esta vez somos nosotros, tú y yo, los aparecidos
a perpetuidad. abajo, pasan los restos de otros barcos y en este
espacio, protegidos de la polución, del desorden y del miedo, una
energía infinita nos desborda, dándonos otra vez forma y medida,
acompañándonos entre estos extraños objetos que nos recibirán.
me siento tan ajena y tan cerca que me asombro ante las puertas,
su barniz, del deterioro del decorado del techo. debió ser una casa
tan bella! —ahora recuerdo mi lento recorrido por Marimbad,
aquella vez, de noche. sueño con figuras de yeso que apenas
tienen movimiento y se desplazan alrededor de una piscina que
si me acerco es de sangre (también me bañaré entre esos tubos
plásticos, sobre la carcomida porcelana de la bañera antigua). a
esta sensación de conocimiento se enrola mi intimidad como a
una vida anterior y soy aquella, que luego, extrañamente, había
renunciado a saber. tú la sigues para convencerme de que esa, al
fin, sin equivocación, soy yo. cargas un cubo de agua (el cubo es de
metal y el líquido se balancea estremecido en su nueva dimensión
de oro blanco). sé que es la nada, la domesticación de este vacío
que no se siente, pero que gira también entre el cortinaje gris
de la escena y nosotros, que nos acercamos lentamente para una
puesta imperfecta: todo el cuerpo preparado para una obediencia

a haunted house on the corner of San Rafael

> ... from room to room they went, hand in
> hand, lifting here, opening there, making sure—
> a ghostly couple...
>
> —Virginia Woolf

a haunted house doesn't reveal its prior encounters easily; it doesn't inform on the intimacy of the couple who inhabits it. clothes hanging from the doors, a half-made bed and a clock continuing at its implacable rhythm. you, you're there when I arrive, and we sit down in two heavy wooden chairs. (I still don't know how the morning light gets in.) my black stockings slide smoothly between your hand and your mouth, covering the foot that you like best. it's cold. she's watching us. he too crosses with my image in the mirror, to remind us that this time we—you and I—are the eternal apparitions. below us, wreckage from other boats floats past, and in this space protected from pollution, from the disorder and fear, an infinite energy flows from us, returning our shape and proportion, accompanying us among these strange objects that will receive us. I feel so remote and so present that I'm frightened by the doors, their varnish, the deteriorating decorations on the ceiling. it was meant to be such a beautiful house!—now I recall my exploration of Marienbad, that time, moving slowly through the city at night. I dream of plaster figurines that hardly move at all yet travel around a pool, and if I come close to that pool, I find it filled with blood (I'll bathe among those plastic tubes, on the rotting porcelain of the antique bathtub). with a sense of familiarity, my intimacy surges up like a prior life, and I'm the woman, who at that time, and strangely, had given up knowledge. you follow her to convince me that I am, finally, unmistakably, her. you carry a cube of water (a cube made of metal; the water balances inside, quivering, in its new dimension of whitened gold). I know it's the nothingness, the domestication of this unrecognized void revolving between us and the gray curtains at the scene, which we slowly approach

sin resurrección; el conocimiento —como un vestido negro— sobre la cama inmensa. cambio esta representación por un día de contemplación. desde los techos decorados; desde la secuencia de los techos que antes fueron dorados, hago un brusco movimiento, frente a la bañera, ante el barniz de esa puerta que da a mi mente —fantasmas indeseables de una casa cuya cortina cerró para nosotros su visibilidad. y aún nos acecha y nos perturba la potencia adquirida; nos culpa y nos reclama volver... casa vampira. te miro, como uno mira los grabados de viejos libros con barcos que se hundirán con sus tesoros al atardecer. no volveremos a ti. un sonido al desplomarse se agudiza en mis oídos: contigo hundiremos también la recalcitrante ilusión de haber estado aquí, cuerpo y sustancia. oficio sin vocación. conciencia de una identidad en mí, en ella, la que condena amparándose en el gesto. no sé que ha querido probar con su desvelo (malograda metafísica, malogrado deseo). yo bajaba una vez más y me unía con mi culpa, con mi incapacidad, buscando siempre una casa en la esquina de mi deseo y ella —lejana desde mi ojo insignificante— se volvía más aparente y más real cada vez, como se vuelve más luminosa la luz que no se desea ver.

with imperfect staging: the entire body prepared for obedience without resurrection; knowledge—like a black dress—sprawled across the enormous bed. I trade this representation for a day of contemplation. from the decorative ceilings, from the sequence of ceilings that once were golden, I make a brusque gesture by the bathtub, at the varnish of the door opening into my mind—undesirable phantoms from a house closed to us behind curtains. and still it stalks us, it unsettles the potency we've acquired; it accuses us and demands our return... vampiric house. I look at you, as one looks at engravings in old books with ships that will sink with their treasures at sundown. we won't come back to you. collapsing, a sound intensifies in my ears: with you we too will flee the stubborn illusion of having been here, body and substance. occupation without a calling. awareness of an identity inside me, inside her, woman taking shelter in her gesture of condemnation. I don't know what she was trying to prove with her efforts (ill-fated metaphysics, ill-fated desire). I went down one more time and merged with my guilt, with my incapacity, always looking for a house on the corner of my desire, and she—far from my insignificant eye—was becoming ever more apparent, ever more real, like light becoming more luminous when you don't want to see it.

imagine (marzo 1990)

ella pintaba con gritos las paredes
para creer que algo estaba allí,
entre el tiempo místico de la creación
y el tiempo del presente
en otra paradoja de la historia
su obsesión constante por lo efímero que ha sido
permanente.
mi ojo, entre el descascaro de la cal
y el reposo
desde un fondo en ocre muy antiguo
y recalcitrante.
del día de Navidad el año 1000
cuando millones de mujeres decoraron sus casas,
los umbrales que fueron barridos por las hojas
pisoteados después
en busca de la divinidad
—termina tu pintura antes que salga el sol—
con polvo de piedra blanca,
con arcilla en valles de hermosa desolación,
o pasta traslúcida hecha con arroz escaldado.
una estatua será engalanada cada día
por una nueva historia
el día de Navidad del año 2000.
se le ofrecerá una guirnalda con flores olorosas
—tal vez leche fresca, miel y ceniza.
y se abrirán los cuerpos de colores
en busca de la divinidad—
se secarán al fuego con la pintura negra
hecha de jugo de fruto malogrado
(todo consistirá en pisotear la hierba
en una misma distancia, en un mismo trayecto)
para que diez mil rosas rojas
formen un macizo tal vez verde
(*Red on Green*, 1992)
el día de Navidad, en África

imagine (March 1990)

she painted the walls with wailing
in order to believe that something was there,
between the mystical time of creation
and the present moment
another paradox of history is
her continual obsession with an ephemeral thing that was
permanent.
my eye, between the peeling of the plaster
and rest
from a background of ancient and
stubborn ochre.
on Christmas Day in the year 1000
when millions of women decorated their houses,
the thresholds were swept clean with leaves
later trodden
in search of divinity
—finish your painting before the sun rises—
with white rock dust,
with clay from handsomely desolate valleys,
or with translucent paste made from scalded rice.
a statue will be adorned each day
with a newborn story
on Christmas Day in the year 2000.
a garland of flowers will be offered
—maybe fresh milk, honey, ashes.
and the corpus of colors will open
in search of divinity—
they'll dry by the fire with black paint
derived from the juices of rotten fruit
(the whole thing will involve treading on the grass
at steady intervals, along a steady path)
so that ten thousand red roses
will become a solid mass, green maybe
(*Red on Green*, 1992)
on Christmas Day in Africa,

donde es más lejos.
capa sobre capa ver cómo se agrieta el color
para formar una especie de borrón, un sueño,
un motivo de confusión entre el motivo
y la superficie
(*Blanquise*, marzo 1991)
también las esculturas de nieve
contienen el frío, la lluvia y la humedad
esa fuerza recalcitrante, en Fairbanks
con cuatro metros de altura
—la noción de máscara, o de figura
se renueva en cada ceremonia del hielo—
y las cosas maduran más allá
del áspero día de la insolación
en el desierto.
la mujer se ha sentado sobre la pintura
y la borra cuidadosamente.
(una mujer dibuja todos los días frente a su casa)
un quetzal
y la tierra nunca ha sido más bella
que en ese instante
en que el pájaro deja una estela en la arena,
en el polvo, en el hielo, en la montaña,
qué más se puede pedir?
el dibujo cambia con nosotros en el día que pasa
y encuentra tus huellas (*Walking*, 1967)
(*Correo de la UNESCO*, en diciembre)
el día de Navidad.

farther away.
layer upon layer see how the color cracks open
to form a kind of sketch, a dream,
the motif of confusion between motif
and surface
(*Blanquise*, March 1991)
and snow sculptures
contain the cold, the rain, and the humidity,
that stubborn force in Fairbanks
four meters high
—the conceit of the mask, or of the figure
is renewed in every ice ceremony—
and things mature beyond
the harsh day of exposure
in the desert.
the woman sat down on the painting
and she erases it carefully.
(every day in front of her home a woman draws)
a quetzal bird
and the earth has never been more beautiful
than in that instant
when the bird leaves a trail on the sand,
in the dust, on the ice, on the mountain,
what more could you ask for?
the drawing changes with us as the day moves on
and discloses your footprints (*Walking*, 1967)
(*The UNESCO Courier*, December)
on Christmas Day.

Interview

Intense Circularities:
An Interview of Reina María Rodríguez by Rosa Alcalá. June 25, 2001. [1]

The following conversation, which took place on the terrace of Casa de Letras, came out of a discussion I had with Ms. Rodríguez and Kristin Dykstra[2] a week earlier in La Azotea, an alternative literary space and the writer's home. After a month in Cuba, I had come to feel that Casa de Letras, a resource for writers and an open space for readings and workshops, was my second home. It was then located in the tower of El Palacio del Segundo Cabo, in the heart of Old Havana. I often stopped by to see who was hanging out, to leave a message for someone I couldn't get a hold of, to give a workshop, to listen to a talk. This center was founded by Ms. Rodríguez and inaugurated with the "Primer Encuentro de Poesía del Lenguaje" (First Conference on Language Poetry) in January 2001—an idea that came up in conversation with Charles Bernstein after she gave a reading for SUNY Buffalo's Wednesdays @ Four Series. A number of writers and artists from Buffalo, as well as all over the U.S., Latin America, and Europe, attended the conference. I returned for the month of June as the assistant to SUNY Buffalo's study abroad program and spent most of my free time with local writers. Looking out over different neighborhoods in Havana, both La Azotea and Casa de Letras were vulnerable to climate and environmental changes, unwilling or unable to shut out neighborhood noise, gossip, the demands and criticism of participants, the wind, flies. Obeying such natural laws, our conversation concluded as the encroaching afternoon sun forced us to call it a day. Our translated interview has been edited and condensed. As Dykstra remarks in the introduction to this book, Rodríguez later changed the name of Casa de Letras to Torre de Letras.

— Rosa Alcalá

---

1   Havana, Cuba. Recorded at Casa de Letras. Originally published in an earlier form in *A.bacus* (Potes & Poets Press, 2002). Reprinted with the permission of Rosa Alcalá.

2   A special thanks to her for clarifying some of the references in this interview that I was unable to decipher, and for offering translation and editing advice.

ROSA ALCALÁ: When we met in La Azotea you were speaking about the maternal space, weren't you?

REINA MARÍA RODRÍGUEZ: Yes, well, if we were to look at this maternal space psychologically, it has to do with the loss of my brother, of my father. My father died young, very young—my brother, too. And I wanted to find a substitute. I also decided to have children. So that must have been one of the causes.

RA: Didn't you already have two children when you started La Azotea?

RMR: I started it when I had Elis.[3] But before that, we would meet downstairs.[4] But the children have always been—how should I say—too few. I would have had more.

RA: Really?

RMR: Yes. I had two *legrados*.[5] One was a decision that affected me tremendously, and the other one was because of a problem with the egg and I couldn't have it—but I would have. I like to give birth. Truthfully, I think it's one of those moments—that very moment of having someone inside of you, and then seeing that person leave, come out of you—it's something I've never written about, but it has made such an impression on me that I would have continued having children. If I'm afraid of anything, it's the inability to have more children.

In any case, what I always do with others is to convert them into characters—it's perhaps what everyone does. Others do it in a less obvious way. Also because the people who have moved towards something with you become fewer and fewer. And the most important thing in

---

3   Her fourth and youngest child, who was almost eleven years old at the time of the interview. Rodríguez has three sons (all, as Antonio José Ponte observes, given names beginning with the letter *E*).

4   At an apartment where her mother lived.

5   *Legrado* refers to a medical procedure which has among its uses the termination of a pregnancy.

friendship is just that, to arrive at a place together. In that respect, there is a wonderful novel, an unfinished novel by René Daumal, called *Mount Analogue*. I read this book many years ago and my ideas about friendship have to do with this book—that trajectory one ascends with another person. And La Azotea, and what we have in Casa de Letras now, comes out of the idea that people should feel like themselves, not as if they are going to some event or to participate in something formal, something not creative. For example, Javier[6] is over there writing his texts on the computer. That's the most important thing one can do for a writer—to give him a place where he can be as he wishes and write. I don't know if I've answered your question. I've always experienced that friendship trauma, and because I always feel that my friends are leaving, I try very hard to keep them. But what I love most always leaves me, and so this is my means of possession, of egoism and power—but it's a power that has nothing to do with the political. It has to do with the uterus.

RA: Do you see your work, your poetry, as a kind of womb, too?

RMR: I think there is an intense circularity. I realize this now—not just because of the very word, but because of the egg, and also because the city itself is enclosed. There is always something that's enclosed, humid. Yes, I believe it has something to do with poetry. Yes, yes.

RA: When I was here in January, you referred to yourself as "bombilla pa' los pollitos"[7] mother hen. What is your relationship with young poets that causes them to be drawn to you and La Azotea?

RMR: Well, it's not a matter of generation or age difference; it's important on a level of essence—to tap into the essence that I find in someone else and that I think already resides in me, and that has something to do with Cuban literature in the last analysis. I say in the last analysis because to just say "Cuban Literature" is to say a lot, it's

6   Javier Marimón.

7   Literally, a "lightbulb for chicks."

something that already belongs to the critics, that belongs to... I feel like it's a thread that weaves its way through Escobar,[8] and Ponte, and Rolando Sánchez Mejías, with a group that can be connected in this way. And I tried to find this textile in us[9] too, but with a bit more difficulty. I think that this generation has—or this group has—many problems of concentration. They are not—they don't pretend to be—intellectuals. And they are also more indifferent. They haven't consciously recognized their identity or potential as a group. And it's like a group that tries to elude any maturation. In the case of Javier, for example, I would have loved for him to have been my own son—not as far as his problems, but because of his work. I've never had a child who writes. I think that Elis writes some very good stories, but she still doesn't know what she wants to be. They've been drawn to mathematics, cybernetics, to another world that is also creative, but I've been left with that [desire for a child who writes]. I love to teach—to give them books that I wish I would have read at their age, but that I read only later. When I read, for example, his book,[10] I felt there was something in it that moved me to write. What matters to me are books that move me to make more books, and that rarely happens with a contemporary. What happens is that their conduct is much more irreverent. But more so, it's as if they were in a state of inertia. It's a lot of work, for example, to create a space for them, because the space that was created in La Azotea was always a very political one, and yet they elude any consideration that is purely political.

RA: Until now, you've spoken of the poets who are here, of old friends, of the new generation, but I've noticed that lately many foreigners have come through here, many students...

RMR: Yes.

---

8   Ángel Escobar.

9   The group of young writers associated with La Azotea and Casa de Letras.

10   She gestures towards Javier Marimón, who is working on the computer a few yards away.

RA: ... from Emory, from Buffalo, people who come to do some research. How do you think La Azotea functions within those kinds of poetic relationships?

RMR: Well, never has La Azotea charged an admission fee for a reading. The reality is that the country has changed, and that there are possibilities for students to come and hear a writer give a talk. A reading provides subsistence for the writers. In other words, I never wanted La Azotea to be a place to give hand-outs, nor that it should turn bureaucratic, or anything like that, because it would create problems among ourselves. Simply, it would be a place to be. But now there is a different situation. If these groups or students, for example, could provide the means so that the speaker not be a functionary but a writer, and that that writer be perhaps someone less valued, in the sense that they don't receive funds to do what they want—they don't have steady jobs and even if they do, it's not enough for even the smallest indulgence. Then, that's the idea I wanted to realize, so that some writers could receive money within this context. Independently and on other occasions, what came out of Buffalo has created a sense of purpose, which is my relationship with all of you, the reason I have the translations. They, for example, the younger ones, are not aware of the importance of a public, of someone making an effort for you, of translating a text. They don't realize how important that is, the value that that has, beyond monetary. It is priceless. That someone would, like Kris,[11] send me an email that says that she found the original English-language source, in a Virginia Woolf story, for a fragment in "a haunted house on the corner of San Rafael." She worries herself with these things; she works with me, and I'm writing for what she can do later with the work. They still have no idea of the value these relationships have. And there is the affective aspect, too, no? For example, when I was in Atlanta,[12] I was sick for the entire week, and so many students came to visit me. And so many of them were weighed down with schoolwork and other things, and they really had little time to dedicate to poetry. And I took with me

---

11   Kristin Dykstra.

12   At Emory University.

Sylvia's[13] poems, which were unpublished, and I ended up publishing them in La Azotea. So now, Sylvia, who is a good poet, begins to be part of that follow-up. We exchange emails. I've maintained a friendship with Néstor.[14] And when they left Havana on Saturday, I was very depressed, because I continue to establish relationships with people who come and go and may never return. In other words, Rosa, I don't believe that literature is territorial. Not only for Cuban literature, but for all literature. The poet has no determined place.

RA: You are going to Iowa now, aren't you?

RMR: I'm going to Iowa.

RA: The poets who are going are all Cubans?

RMR: Yes, Cubans. But María Mercedes[15] is also going, and Néstor. But any number of people are attending because they want to see us again.

RA: And that will be with the Spanish department?

RMR: The department of literature.

RA: And these are all people that have some relationship to you here, no?

RMR: Yes.

RA: Do you think that La Azotea was useful in some way to inform others outside of Cuba about certain issues?

RMR: I believe so. Everyone has made do[16] however they can, but at cer-

---

13   Sylvia Figueroa, then a graduate student in Emory's Spanish department.

14   Néstor Rodríguez, also at Emory at that time.

15   María Mercedes Carrión.

16   She uses the word "resolver," to resolve, which is often applied to describe the various creative techniques with which Cubans survive their economic limitations.

tain moment, La Azotea was important because it produced eleven anthologies. Whether you like anthologies or not—I, for example, don't like them—the fact that there are ten or eleven anthologies, some of them bilingual, indicates an acknowledgement. Many people, many critics, have passed through there. And that gave it, to a certain extent, an image. I was very afraid that an image would be created and that what was produced there could not live up to that image. As a result, when I began to see that it was becoming an image, and that there were no longer the people to sustain it, then I began to feel it was a fraud. I don't want that image to fill up with bubbles, so that what is happening does not measure up. La Azotea is now a bit of a spectacle, I believe that, more than ever. It is a place where we do something that has more to do with the past, but that no longer moves us to discovery as naturally as it did years ago. But again, the relationships between all of those people who used to be in La Azotea and who are no longer here, compared to those who are, have changed, because that place has changed, and it has continued to change. It's constantly being negotiated. But the photos still remain in La Azotea. I wouldn't want to convert that into La Bodeguita del Medio.[17] I would never want the exploitation of that place, because it is also my home. And what I want in my house is the memory of those who were once there, and that memory cannot be manipulated. In other words, if the time comes when we install four tables and start charging for tea, the moment when it is converted into something like that, then it will be too much of a tourist trap. It will lose whatever significance it has.

If they were to give me a house with a swimming pool in Miramar,[18] I would never go. My house is the one I built, with the materials I gathered myself, with that hole I fix a little bit each day. And it is literature that has allowed me to do that, but I would never do it, I would never try to embellish it in order to change it into something it's not.

RA: In either a negative or positive way, how do you feel that La Azotea

---

17   A famous bar and tourist destination in Havana.

18   A wealthy neighborhood in Havana.

intervenes in or interrupts your work?

RMR: Completely. I think that it almost completely interrupts [my work]. Yesterday, in order to recuperate the days that I spent with you, and that I was here in the Casa de Letras, or somewhere else, I had to return to reading and I felt that emptiness, the feeling of that empty house. And to return to that state is always difficult, it causes depression, it's difficult to re-establish a rhythm. Today I've come out trying to capture that rhythm I once had—the same thing happened to me in January,[19] when so many people came. I think it's an addiction. I think it has to do with a guilt complex because I've been given so much. I think I've been given something I want to share… To think that perhaps I'm doing this out of generosity or because I'm a good person would make me feel even more guilty. Since I don't want to continue that chain of guilt complexes, I want to share what has been given to me and what I've always had, and the more I share, the more I will have, because I've always had more, that's my problem. The same happens to me with everything, with my clothes, with my personal belongings—of course, there came a time when I gave away so much that I found myself completely broke.

RA: How does this affect your relationship with Topo,[20] with…?

RMR: It affects… well, Elis. I dedicate as much time as I can to her, Rosa. She'll soon be eleven years old, and of those years, I've dedicated myself to her as much as possible. For example, the other day she said to me, you spent all these days away, now you will have to take me to rehearsal. We went to rehearsal, I picked her up, I waited for her… I try, for example, to talk to her a lot. I know that there is tension between us because she wants to dismantle whatever power I have over her, and that has to do with her age. With Topo, he also gets tired, he's tired because sometimes there are too many people, but since he also

---

19   The First Encounter of Language Poetry conference in Casa de Letras, 2001.

20   Nickname for Jorge Miralles, her former domestic partner. Miralles went on to win UNEAC's Premio David for his book, *Las voces del pantano*.

doesn't know what he needs his silence for... or should I say, he's still not sure what he will do with it, what he will accomplish. He's trying to write a novel. And also because he's also a very tyrannical person, very possessive. He seems to be the opposite, but truly, what he appears to be, he is not. Topo is more tyrannical and possessive with me than I am with him. So then, there was a time when we were very alone, there was no one, everyone had left, and that became a mutual construction—there, there, there—alone. And that created a kind of territory that you don't want anyone to enter. And so then La Azotea has caused... My friends are his friends. He has no other space, no other friends. He always feels that it's a place that isn't his place, that he has friends who are not his friends, that he plays second fiddle here. And that, to a certain extent, affects him.

I don't have, nor do I want, any type of power in Casa de Letras. I don't want to direct anything. If I had wanted to do cultural work in this country, I would have become the Vice-Minister of Culture. I would have taken some position and I've refused. I don't want to make any money off of this. I do it as an addiction. Like a smoker, it's an addiction. It's an addiction to promoting, to collaborating with others—it has something to do with sociability. It's that and at the same time, it's the complete opposite. When I'm too absorbed in that state for too long, it immediately produces a feeling of terror, and I want to do something else. It's damaging. It's not beneficial because it detracts from my work, but it's also my justification for what I don't accomplish. I finished my novel, that left me exhausted, and there was a need to seed, create something new. And now here I began to shoot the photos for my book on Havana.

On Saturday I listened to some very good Cuban music that Ponte brought to my house, and suddenly, I really enjoyed it, because I was there in that moment with the person who brought the music. And sometimes I do things in that way, but other times I'm concerned with making a "set"—and I think there's always an artist producing a "set." It hurts me and it makes me very tired. Sometimes I arrive home very, very tired—not because of the work itself, but because of the work of

representation, the constant simulation that it requires. Because of its window dressing. It's a performance.

RA: What do you see as La Azotea's future?

RMR: Well, I always want to contain what is most intimate, which has to do with spaces in which to converse and feel at home. Even though it may be more taxing, I like to prepare tea, tend to guests, all of that. I'd rather have La Azotea be that—to conserve that aspect of it. Of course, never with any type of programming. Very open. Letting things be as they are, not changing them. And this place, what it has—its very location, the tower, the view—just kills me. I come here and I can write, peacefully. Sometimes it has a frigidity that happens when things are altered, when they are too touristy. But, for example, looking at that bell, there is a black bird that perches on the weathervane, and he has a bunch of poems written about him, because what matters to me is the sound and the black bird and that weathervane, which is a reproduction, it is not the original. And then, the well is dirty, it's murky, it's filled with all of the things that have fallen into it. Sometimes it's cleaned, but I like it because it's dirty, because it's contaminated. There is a branch that I spend all of my time thinking about when I'm here in the morning, or I think about how the bay changes color, about El Cristo.[21] There are places that I'm attracted to for certain reasons, and I'm not sure why, but it seems that terraced roofs interest me, and this is also one. I convert all landscapes into text—it is a kind of use, but it's the only use I can give it, because my life is nothing more than that. It is not a contemplative life; it is simply a life to steal from one place and take to another. As long it produces this feeling, I'll continue to come here. And to leave a cottage behind. To leave some books here, some workshops, to let people come here and feel like they are in that other tower—the one they call the ivory tower, or the "university for some" or the "university for none."[22] It is the place where Javier can

---

21 The Estatua de Cristo (Statue of Christ) is at Casablanca, across the harbor from Old Havana's Plaza de Armas. The statue can be seen from the terrace of Casa de Letras.

22 "Universidad para Todos" ("University for Everyone") is a government project that uses mass media to teach university courses to the Cuban population.

work, and Richard[23] can come and talk about Brazilian literature. Or anyone else. Omar[24] can do his I Ching. I see all of this. He can do that in his own house, but he'll show up with his I Ching wrapped in a cloth, and he takes it out of a black velvet container, and that type of environment nourishes me.

RA: Do you see this "azotea" as a satellite of the other?

RMR: No, it's like an offshoot, but it's different. This place will never be that place—what that was cannot even be described. At a time when there was nothing, that was a place to be, and people would come, they would bathe, eat, sleep. Rogelio[25] would say to me: "Please turn off the telephone because I haven't slept all night and I'm going to stay here"—because he worked as a night watchman—"I'm going to stay here and I don't want the phone to bother me." And so I would make it my duty to see that Rogelio get some sleep. And that was my life.

And here, I've tried to reproduce that. But here I have money to buy books, to have a library. I've yet to find someone who could later direct this. I think that person needs to be constructed. He has to desire it very much; he has to do it because he really wants to do it; and also, he must have the humility required by this position. It's a priesthood. That I don't see it as a satellite also has to do with the fact that I don't want to sell it. I don't want to. I want people to read here. To feel comfortable when they read. So when they look at La Habana, they see not just La Habana for tourists, but one that belongs to them. And so this place will have the tranquility a writer needs, and so music can be played, so they can hear the music they like—just some resources, I don't think it's too much to ask. Above all, to have the books a writer needs, according to what some writers might... I can't do this by quantity, or by following statistics. I've gathered recommendations from

---

23 Ricardo Alberto Pérez.

24 Omar Pérez.

25 Rogelio Saunders.

Ponte, Antón[26] —my own, from others—and those are the books that are going to be here—arbitrarily, because these books are not academic and they are not classified in the sense of representing an absolute power deciding what a writer must read. Really, no academy, no school, would be able to decide that.

RA: How were you able to obtain this place?

RMR: Abel[27] had someone show me this place, and I came and saw that it was full of junk... garbage. It used to be a publishing house, but they were moving. I just froze—I said, "This is the place," and we immediately began to remove the garbage. Even on the day of its inauguration, we were still painting the little stairs—that very day. I still don't know how it can be real. I went to the place where furniture can be purchased by government check and they didn't have what I wanted. I wanted a glass cabinet. Those cabinets can be bought in pesos, but they must be bought individually, and not by voucher. And so I had to accommodate the vision of what I wanted to what was available in those places where I could purchase them. In other words, nothing here is perfect, because those bookcases were not the ones I wanted, but I bought them. Now I'm having some photos of writers and philosophers framed. The photos also aren't perfect—they are photos ripped out of old, used books. I don't know if it can be achieved, but to bring, for example, a sunflower here gives me a loving feeling, like being in a temple, a place where something can be achieved. Like Cuban literature once was: in gardens, in small and discreet places, intimate places. If I convert this place into a series of activities, then I make it ordinary. What good is it to have a computer and a photocopier if it's merely a place to promote functionaries and their ideas about culture? No, I want this to be what we really want. But it's a lot of work. It takes up a lot of my time.

RA: So then, when do you write?

---

26   Antón Arrufat.

27   Prieto, Minister of Culture.